Be an Explorer. Not a Tourist.

…And Travel With Integrity.

It feels good to support the people and places in this book.
We are about to introduce you to good people,
good places and good businesses that deserve your time.

ALEXA WEST GUIDES

Vietnam, New Edition 2023

Copyright © 2023 The Solo Girl's Travel Guide

All rights reserved. No part of this publication may be reproduced or copied or transmitted in any form, physical or electronic, or recorded without prior permission from The Solo Girl's Travel Guide ™

Please contact us at hello@thesologirlstravelguide.com

The Solo Girl's Travel Guide updates this book series year-round, as businesses grow, change, and even sometimes, close. A quick double-check before you drive an hour to a restaurant is always a safe practice - as these things are out of our control. And hey, if you see a change we should know about – we'd love it if you let us know so we can update our guide for future travelers.

STOCK OUR BOOK

Want to stock our book in your shop, store, or platform? Send us a message at hello@thesologirlstravelguide.com

the SOLO GIRL'S TRAVEL GUIDE

VIETNAM

ALEXA WEST GUIDES

EVERY GIRL SHOULD TRAVEL SOLO AT LEAST ONCE IN HER LIFE

You don't need a boyfriend, a travel partner or anyone's approval to travel the world. And you don't need a massive bank account or an entire summer off work.

All you need is that wanderlust in your blood and a good guidebook in your hands.

If you've doubted yourself for one moment, remember this:

Millions of girls travel across the globe all by themselves every damn day and you can, too.

You are just as capable, just as smart, and just as brave as the rest of us. You don't need permission – this is your life.

Listen to your gut, follow your heart and remember that the best adventures start with the simple decision to go.

TRAVEL FAR ENOUGH TO MEET YOURSELF.

What travelers are saying...

"Vietnam was one of the most memorable trips of my life to date! Luckily, I picked up this book before I jetted off to the fusion of French and Asian cuisine and the bustling cities of Saigon and Hanoi. This book was full of helpful tips and made me feel more confident as I stepped off the plane to experience Vietnam! I highly recommend it!"

- Andrea

"Best travel guide! I love Alexa West travel guides. I've bought 4 now and they have helped me plan my trips with ease and safety. I've planned group trips with her books and she makes sure to list a range of things to do to please everyone. I always get compliments about the trips I plan but I owe it all to her travel guide. Her books are like hiring someone to plan it all for you but at a fraction of the cost!"

- Alisha

"This book was awesome. Very easy to understand and read and figure out where to go eat and visit. I actually took her advice and went to the places in the book and she was spot on. I even reached out to the driver she used and he was the sweetest nicest honest person you could ever meet. She definitely made traveling easy. I enjoyed my trip and I brought the book with me."

- Travelgirlaz

"This Vietnam travel guide is wonderful - well written and researched, clearly and practically guiding you through an overview of the country and possible journeys and adventures that await. It has detailed information on every city, including those not on the beaten path, and of course, pertinent information specifically for women travelers around our safety and health. Highly recommended!"

- Jessica

Nice to meet you! I'm Lexi...

I'm not here to get rich or reach 1 million followers on Instagram. I'm here because I want to change the way we travel as women. I want to empower you to travel with less fear and more fun all while avoiding the scams, creeps, and sketchy hangouts. I want you to go into this trip confident enough to let your guard down outside of your comfort (and time) zone.

And I do that by connecting you to the most beautiful places, the kindest people, the most challenging opportunities, and the most rewarding experiences that have the Solo Girl Stamp of Approval. All the things you're about to read are approved by me. I would send my little sister to these places. But since I don't have a little sister, you're my little sister (even if you're older than me). So trust me to guide you on one of the most life-changing journeys you'll ever have!

This trip. This is when you discover exactly who you are.

A LITTLE ABOUT ME

Back in 2010, I was a broke-ass Seattle girl who had just graduated from college and had about $200 to my name. I was faced with two choices: get a job, a husband, and have 3 babies plus a mortgage…or sell everything I owned and travel the world.

Obviously, I made the right choice.

For the past 10+ years, I've been traveling the world solo. I've played every travel role from being the young volunteer and broke backpacker to flying to exotic islands to review new luxury hotels and give breath to struggling tourism industries.

Now I spend my days as an explorer on a mission to change the way that women travel the world. I want to show you places you've never seen and unlock hidden doors you never knew existed in places you may have been before. I want to create a path for you where you feel safe while diving deeper into cultures and countries beyond your own – whether for a week, a year, or a lifetime. And that's what I'm doing.

xoxo, Alexa West

FIND MY VIETNAM PLAYLIST HERE

Flights, airports, walking around town…

Travel is a little bit more magical when good music is involved.

 # Don't forget your map!

You will find maps in this book - but general maps to give you general ideas. For detailed maps on your phone that will ACTUALLY help you find the things in this book, follow these steps:

1. Scan the QR Code.

2. Once the map opens up in your Google Maps, it's automatically saved in your account!

3. Browse. Get a mental idea of where is what.

4. To find your map just tap on Saved on the bottom bar, and then on Maps, on the bottom right of your screen.

Now you're prepared.

Bonus! Download GoogleMaps Offline like this…

Step 1: Open GoogleMaps

Step 2: In the search bar, type "Okay Maps".

Step 3: Select the vicinity to download (usually a city or neighborhood) and click download.

WANT MORE TRAVEL TIPS?

Join Alexa's travel tip email series. This will change how you travel forever.

Go to Alexa-West.com and sign-up for the newsletter.

THE CONTENTS

Introduction to Vietnam 11
A Quick Breakdown
of Vietnam 14
A Quick History of Vietnam 19
Vietnam 101 21
The Mini Vietnam Bucket List 25
The Mini Food & Drink
Bucket List 29

How to Explore the
Best of Vietnam 30
   Quick Itineraries for Vietnam 31
   Transportation in Vietnam 35

Vietnam Survival Guide 39
   Visas for Vietnam 40
   Weather for Vietnam 42
   Vietnamese Food Guide 45
   Vietnamese Language Guide 49
   What to Pack 52
   How to Budget 55
   Internet & Data 58
   Crime & Safety 59
   Do's & Dont's 60

Chapter 1: Hanoi 65
   Introduction to Hanoi 66
   Areas to Explore 68
   Where to Stay 70
   Where to Stay 73
   Nightlife 78
   Sightseeing 81
   Markets & Shopping 88
   Beauty & Wellness Guide 91
   From the Airport to Hanoi 93

Chapter 2: Ha Giang 95
   Introduction to Ha Giang 96
   What to Pack for Ha Giang 99

Chapter 3: Sapa 100
   Introduction to Sapa 101
   Areas to Know 103
   Where to Stay 106
   Where to Stay 110
   Nightlife 111
   Best Things to Do in Sapa 112
   Markets & Shopping 117
   Crime & Safety 118
   Insider Tips for Sapa 119
   How to Get to Sapa 120

Chapter 4: Halong Bay
or Lan Ha Bay? 124
   Lan Ha Bay 126
   Halong Bay 128

Chapter 5: Ninh Binh 130
   Introduction to Ninh Binh 131
   Areas to Know 132
   Where to Stay 133
   Where to Eat 135
   Drinking & Nightlife 137
   Things to Do 138
   How to Get Around 143

Chapter 6: Phong Nha 144
   Introduction Phong Nha 145
   How to Spend Your Time
   in Phong Nha 146
   Where to Stay 149
   Where to Eat 152
   Things to Do in Phong Nha 154
   How to Move Around
   Phong Nha 155
   How to Get to Phong Nha 156

Chapter 7: Hue 157

Introduction to Hue 158
Areas to Know 160
Where to Stay 161
Where to Eat 163
Nightlife & Fun 165
Culture & Tours 166
Sightseeing 167
More Fun Things to Do 170
Markets & Shopping 174
How to Get Around Hue 175
Scams Particularly in Hue 176

Chapter 8: Hoi An Ancient City ... 178
Introduction to
Hoi An Ancient City 179
Areas to Know 180
Where to Stay 182
Where to Eat 185
Drinking & Nightlife 190
Things to Do & See 191
Markets & Shopping 194
Beauty & Wellness 195
How to Get Around 197

Chapter 9: Hoi An Beach 198
Introduction to Hoi An Beach 199
Areas to Know 200
Where to Stay 202
Where to Eat 205
Things to Do 207
How to Get Around 209
How to Get to Hoi An Beach 210

Chapter 10: Da Nang 211
Introduction to Da Nang 212
Areas to Know 213
Where to Stay 215
Where to Eat 217
Things to Do 219
Sightseeing & Culture 221
Daytrips from Da Nang 222

Chapter 11: Mui Ne 223

Introduction to Mui Ne 224
Areas to Know 225
Where to Stay 226
Where to Stay 228
Fun Things to Do 229
Markets & Shopping 231
How to Get Around 232

Chapter 12: Dalat 233
Introduction to Dalat 234
Areas to Explore 235
Where to Stay 237
Where to Eat 239
Nightlife in Dalat 242
Sightseeing & Adventures 243
Shopping in Dalat 246

Chapter 13:
Ho Chi Minh City 247
Ho Chi Minh City 248
Areas to Explore 250
Best Tours in 254
Where to Stay 256
Where to Eat 258
Bars & Nightlife 263
History & Culture 265
Fun Things to Do 269
Markets & Shopping 271
How to Get Around 273
From the Airport
to Ho Chi Minh City 274

Mini Vietnam Directory 276
The 11 Travel Commandments 280
Solo Girl's Travel Guide 280

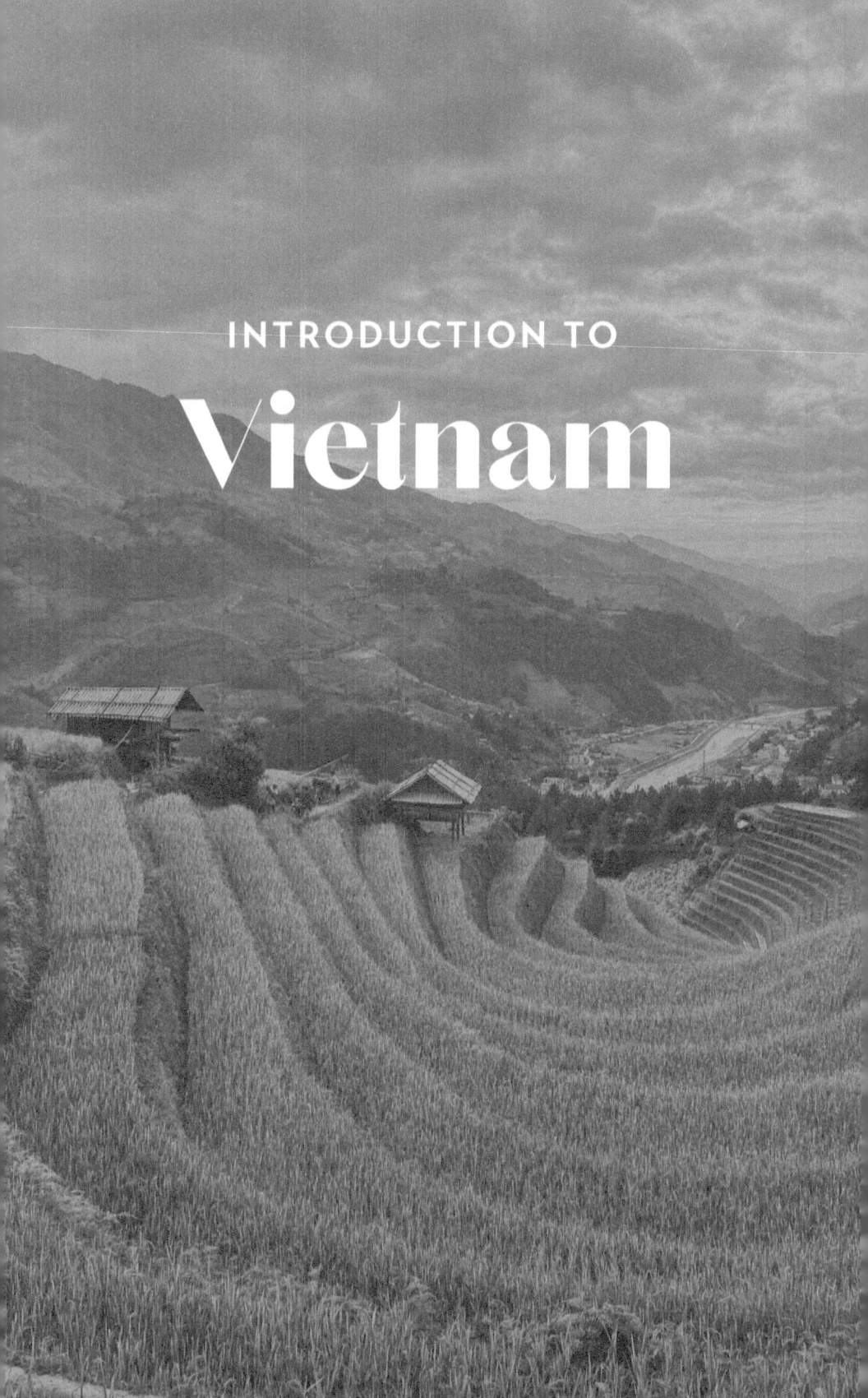

INTRODUCTION TO
Vietnam

WELCOME TO VIETNAM

Journey from north to south of Vietnam and you'll feel like you're traveling through 50 distinct worlds all within the borders of one nation. Often associated with iconic images of rice fields, straw hats, and reminders of past conflicts, however, there is so much more to this captivating country that goes beyond agriculture and historical tragedies.

Vietnam's modern cities, like Ho Chi Minh City and Hanoi, are dynamic metropolises that offer an exciting blend of contemporary lifestyle and cultural heritage. Get ready to be swept up in the energy of bustling markets, trendy rooftop bars, and world-class dining experiences, while still being able to explore historical landmarks and immerse yourself in the country's rich traditions.

Vietnam's modern amenities go hand in hand with its thrilling outdoor activities. Whether it's exploring the world's largest caves in Phong Nha, kitesurfing in Mui Ne, trekking in the Northern mountains, or diving in the crystal-clear waters of Phu Quoc, adventure seekers will find a wide array of thrilling experiences to choose from.

As you will soon see, Vietnam is a book that absolutely needs a guide. Hold on tight.

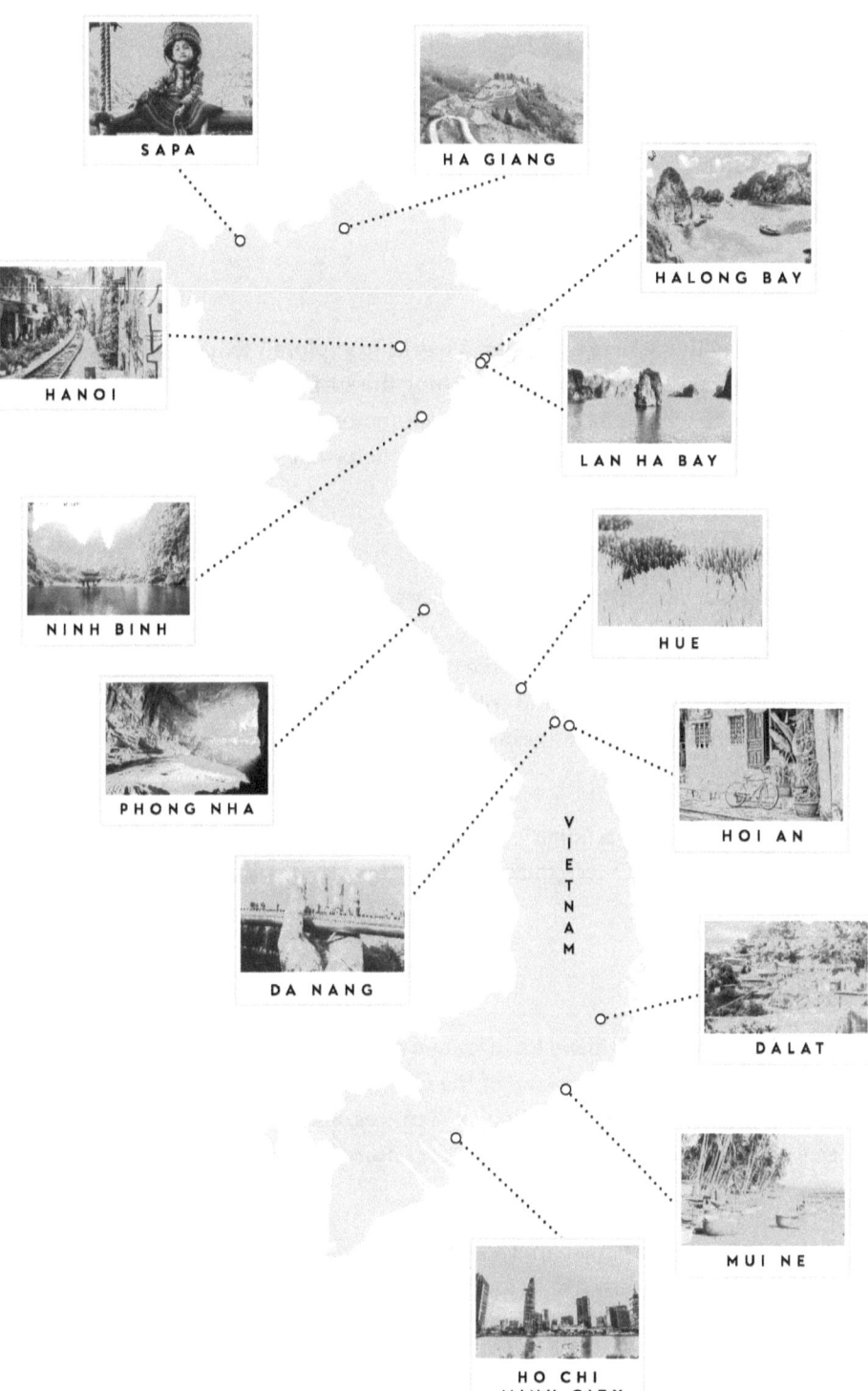

INTRODUCTION TO VIETNAM

A Quick Breakdown of Vietnam

I always say that you need at least 4 weeks to explore Vietnam properly - but even then, 4 weeks is just scratching the surface. Let me give you a little teaser to which cities, towns and mountainous regions we will cover in this book so you can skip right to the sections that speak to you.

1. HA GIANG

Ha Giang is a paradise for nature enthusiasts, boasting stunning landscapes of terraced rice fields, limestone plateaus, and winding mountain roads. It offers an authentic glimpse into the traditional lives of ethnic minorities. Majestic mountain passes and rolling hills create a picturesque setting, perfect for trekking and motorbike adventures.

FUN FACT! Ha Giang is home to the mesmerizing Dong Van Karst Plateau Geopark, a UNESCO-recognized global geopark with unique geological features.

2. SAPA

Sapa is a charming highland town known for its vibrant hill tribes, colorful markets, and panoramic views of the Hoang Lien Son mountain range. The lush green valleys, cascading rice terraces, and picturesque trekking trails make Sapa an ideal destination for nature lovers and hikers.

FUN FACT! Mount Fansipan, located near Sapa, is the highest peak in Indochina, often referred to as the "Roof of Indochina."

3. HANOI

The capital city of Vietnam, Hanoi, seamlessly blends ancient heritage with modernity. It entices visitors with its rich history, delectable street food, and vibrant Old Quarter.

While Hanoi is a bustling city, the peaceful Hoan Kiem Lake and the serene West Lake offer tranquil oases amidst the urban chaos.

FUN FACT! Hanoi boasts the Temple of Literature, Vietnam's first university, dating back to 1070, and is dedicated to Confucius.

4. HA LONG BAY & LAN HA BAY

These UNESCO World Heritage Sites present a surreal seascape of thousands of limestone karsts and islets, adorned with emerald waters and hidden caves. Cruising through Ha Long Bay or kayaking on Lan Ha Bay unveils a mesmerizing blend of nature and ancient legend.

FUN FACT! Ha Long Bay's name translates to "Descending Dragon Bay," derived from a legend about dragons helping protect Vietnam from invaders by spitting out jade and gems that turned into islands.

5. NINH BINH

Often referred to as "Halong Bay on Land," Ninh Binh features breathtaking landscapes of limestone formations, lush greenery, and tranquil waterways. The region's karst formations and river valleys make it a serene haven for boat trips, hiking, and exploring ancient temples.

FUN FACT! The 2017 Hollywood blockbuster "Kong: Skull Island" was filmed in the scenic landscapes of Ninh Binh.

6. PHONG NHA

Phong Nha is a haven for adventurers and explorers, home to one of the world's largest cave systems, including the famous Son Doong Cave. Underground rivers, impressive stalactites, and vast chambers create a surreal subterranean wonderland for cave enthusiasts.

FUN FACT! Son Doong Cave is so large that it even has its own unique ecosystem, complete with jungles, beaches and weather patterns.

7. HUE

As the former imperial capital of Vietnam, Hue is a treasure trove of historical landmarks, including the iconic Imperial City. The Perfume River flows through Hue, offering peaceful boat rides and scenic views of the surrounding countryside.

FUN FACT: Hue's Imperial City was the home of the Nguyen Dynasty, the last ruling family of Vietnam.

8. HOI AN:

Hoi An enchants visitors with its well-preserved ancient architecture, lantern-lit streets, and artistic ambiance. The nearby Cua Dai and An Bang beaches offer relaxation and stunning coastal scenery.

FUN FACT: Hoi An was a bustling international trading port in the 16th and 17th centuries, and its multicultural influences are reflected in its architecture and cuisine.

9. DANANG:

On the way to or from Hoi An, I come to Dangang for one thing: the night markets and nighttime food culture. Oh, also for the airport which connects to most main cities within Vietnam and Southeast Asia. A hub for expats and digital nomads, Danang is becoming increasingly more westernized but has held onto its culture.

FUN FACT: The Dragon Bridge, an iconic symbol of Danang, is not just a bridge; it breathes fire and water during its weekend shows, adding a touch of magic to the city's skyline.

10. MUI NE:

Mui Ne is a coastal resort town renowned for its unique sand dunes, great wind conditions for water sports, and vibrant fishing village atmosphere. The White and Red Sand Dunes create a surreal desert-like landscape, offering thrilling activities like sandboarding and ATV rides.

FUN FACT: Mui Ne's Red Sand Dunes look even more spectacular during sunrise and sunset, when the shifting colors create a magical atmosphere.

11. DALAT:

Known as the "City of Eternal Spring," Dalat's cooler climate, beautiful flower gardens, and French-inspired architecture make it a popular destination to just wander, sip coffee and eat a bowl of warm pho on a chilly evening.

FUN FACT: Dalat is famous for producing high-quality fruits, vegetables, and flowers, thanks to its temperate climate.

12. HO CHI MINH CITY:

The bustling metropolis of Ho Chi Minh City, formerly Saigon, is Vietnam's economic and cultural heart, brimming with history, modernity, and a vibrant street food scene. Although an urban jungle, the city boasts green parks and the iconic Saigon River, perfect for leisurely boat cruises.

FUN FACT: The War Remnants Museum in Ho Chi Minh City provides a poignant reminder of the Vietnam War and its aftermath.

13. CAN THO:

As the heart of the Mekong Delta, Can Tho is renowned for its floating markets, picturesque canals, and warm hospitality. Exploring the lively floating markets and meandering waterways offers an immersive experience of the Mekong Delta's unique way of life.

FUN FACT: Can Tho's Cai Rang Floating Market is one of the largest and most iconic floating markets in Vietnam, where boats are piled high with fresh produce and goods.

14. PHU QUOC

The biggest and most popular tropical island in Vietnam Is Phu Quoc, famous for its idyllic beaches, crystal-clear waters, and lush jungles. With its coral reefs, dense forests, and mangrove swamps, Phu Quoc offers nature enthusiasts ample opportunities for snorkeling, diving, and exploring the island's diverse ecosystem. It's an ideal getaway for those seeking sun and scuba diving…but this is also what makes Phu Quoc such a touristy destination. It is beautiful…but still, I recommend skipping Phu Quoc unless you're a scuba diver. Instead, for island life, I recommend buying a quick, cheap flight over to Thailand.

FUN FACT: Phu Quoc is the largest island in Vietnam, often referred to as the "Pearl Island," and is renowned for its production of high-quality fish sauce, a staple in Vietnamese cuisine.

FUN FACT! 29.6% of the country does not practice any religion.

INTRODUCTION TO VIETNAM

A Quick History of Vietnam

Once upon a time, in the land of stunning landscapes and resilient people, there emerged the country we know today as Vietnam. Over the past 100 years, this nation has experienced triumphs, tragedies, and a spirit of perseverance that has shaped its vibrant history.

In the early 20th century, Vietnam found itself under the grip of French colonial rule. But the courageous Vietnamese people, led by iconic figures like Ho Chi Minh, began to rise against the oppressors. The struggle for independence reached its climax in 1945 when Ho Chi Minh declared the establishment of the Democratic Republic of Vietnam.

The 1950s marked a tumultuous era as the world witnessed the First Indochina War. Vietnam, along with its neighboring countries, fought against the French for liberation. Eventually, in 1954, the Geneva Accords were signed, granting independence to Vietnam and temporarily dividing the nation into North and South.

The 1960s brought a new chapter in Vietnam's history — the Second Indochina War, commonly known as the Vietnam War. The conflict escalated as the United States intervened to support South Vietnam against the communist forces of the North. The war ravaged the country and caused immense suffering, but the Vietnamese people showcased their indomitable spirit.

Finally, in 1975, after years of relentless struggle, the North Vietnamese forces emerged victorious. The country was reunified under a communist government, and Saigon, the capital of South Vietnam, was renamed Ho Chi Minh City, honoring the beloved leader of the revolution.

The post-war era presented a challenging period for Vietnam. The country faced economic difficulties, but it embarked on a path of reform and gradually shifted towards a market-oriented economy, opening doors for international trade and foreign investment. This transformation marked the beginning of Đổi Mới, Vietnam's economic renovation, in the late 1980s.

Throughout the 1990s and early 2000s, Vietnam experienced remarkable economic growth. The country embraced globalization, attracting foreign investors, and became a hub for manufacturing and export-oriented industries. Tourists flocked to the country to witness its breathtaking landscapes, rich culture, and warm hospitality.

In recent years, Vietnam has continued to thrive economically, emerging as one of the fastest-growing economies in Southeast Asia. It has strengthened its position on the global stage, hosting international events and establishing diplomatic relations with numerous countries.

Today, Vietnam stands as a nation that blends tradition with modernity. Its bustling cities boast skyscrapers and technology hubs, while its rural areas retain the timeless charm of rice fields and picturesque villages. Vietnamese cuisine has gained worldwide recognition, tempting taste buds with its diverse flavors, from mouth watering pho to crispy banh mi.

As we reflect on the past 100 years of Vietnam's history, we witness a nation that has overcome immense challenges, united its people, and positioned itself as a dynamic force in the region. With each passing year, Vietnam continues to evolve, guided by the indomitable spirit of its people and their unwavering determination to build a prosperous future.

And thus, the story of Vietnam continues, with its vibrant history serving as a testament to the strength and resilience of its people — a story that will inspire generations to come.

INTRODUCTION TO VIETNAM

Vietnam 101

THE QUICK FACTS

Language: Vietnamese

Population: Approximately 97 Million People

Total Area: 331,212 sq km (comparable to the size of Germany)

Currency: Vietnamese Dong

Time Zone: Indochina Time (ICT, GMT+7)

Religion: Officially none, but very spiritual.

Where: Vietnam is located on the eastern coast of the Indochinese Peninsula in Southeast Asia. It shares borders with China to the north, Laos and Cambodia to the west, and the South China Sea to the east, with a coastline stretching over 3,260 kilometers.

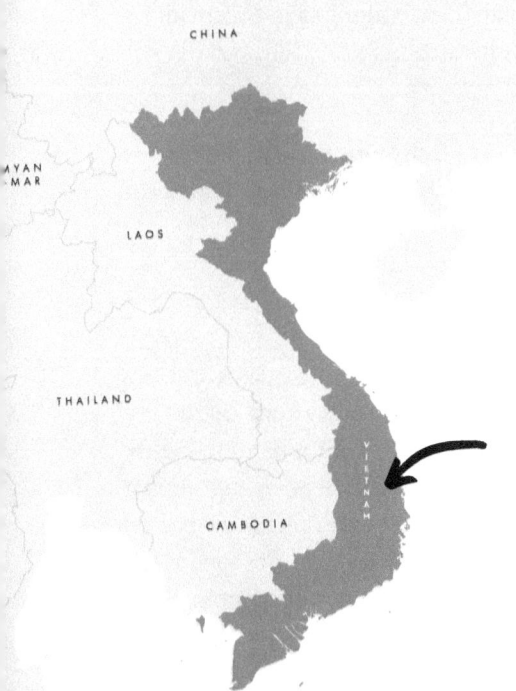

FUN FACT! There are 54 different ethnic groups in Vietnam. Each group has its own dialect and culture. 86% of the population are considered Vietnamese or Kinh, and the remaining 14% belong to different ethnics that are scattered through the highland areas.

THE FOOD

Vietnamese cuisine can be broadly categorized into three regional styles: North, Central, and South, each offering unique flavors and culinary traditions. In the northern region of Vietnam, the cuisine is heavily influenced by Chinese cooking techniques and flavors. The dishes tend to be milder and less sweet compared to other regions, emphasizing light broths and subtle seasonings. On the other hand, southern Vietnamese cuisine, shaped by its tropical climate and proximity to Cambodia and Thailand, is characterized by bold, sweet, and spicy flavors. The dishes often incorporate more herbs, chili peppers, and fermented sauces, resulting in a richer and more intense taste profile. The central cuisine is a mix of both...but with more seafood.

THE PEOPLE

With a population of over 97 million, the people here are known for their strong family values, respect for traditions, deep sense of community and neverending hustle. Education is highly valued, and the younger generation is embracing technology and innovation, driving Vietnam's rapid digital transformation. Vietnam actually produces an impressive amount of millionaires per capita. Whether living in bustling cities or rural areas, the Vietnamese people exhibit a spirit of entrepreneurialism, and a deep connection to their roots. As my Hanoian friend Cuong says, "Vietnamese are entrepreneurs by nature" and you'll see it.

FUN FACT! Vietnam is home to the world's fastest-growing population of ultra-rich individuals with 5,900 millionaires and 260 multimillionaires to date.

YOU & THE PEOPLE

Vietnam's relationship with tourism dates back several decades, attracting travelers from around the world. The reception you receive from Vietnamese people can vary depending on the location's level of tourism. In highly touristy areas, some locals may view travelers as part of a constant stream of visitors and show less enthusiasm. However, venturing off the beaten path, even just a few blocks away from the main tourist hubs, opens the door to encounters with warm and hospitable Vietnamese people. Their genuine hospitality may surprise you, as they invite you into their homes for meals, share cultural experiences, or show you hidden gems in their communities. While some Vietnamese people may see you primarily as a tourist, many are eager to extend a warm welcome.

THE CRIME

Vietnam is generally a safe country for travelers. Tourism is a crucial part of the nation's economy, and therefore, tourists are not typically targeted for random acts of violence. Petty crimes like pickpocketing and minor overcharging may occur, so it's important to remain vigilant and take necessary precautions - but it's nothing to lose sleep over. Traveling solo across the country, even to remote towns and islands, is generally considered safe. Vietnam's safety record surpasses many other parts of the world and this guide will steer you clear of any potentially unsafe areas. You're in good hands.

THE RELIGION

Officially, Vietnam does not have a religion. They're communist, afterall, and the communist government has declared them an atheist state. However, Vietnamese people are very spiritual. The religious influence you will find in Vietnam is mostly Buddhism with influences from Confucianism, Taoism, and indigenous beliefs. Religious observances are cherished occasions. During Buddhist holidays like Vesak, individuals strive to cleanse their minds and perform acts of kindness. So while you'll find pagodas and folklore abound, there is officially no religion here.

THE VOLTAGE

In Vietnam, the voltage is 220 volts. If you're from the US or UK, your curling iron and hair dryer may not work without a voltage converter, but basic electronic devices will function normally. Electric outlets commonly feature Type A and Type C sockets, so make sure to bring the appropriate adaptors for your devices.

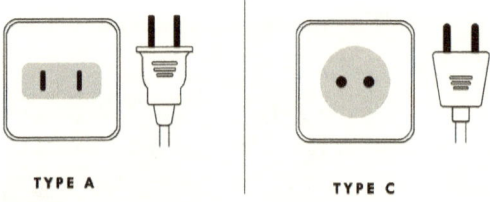

TYPE A   TYPE C

Unless you're carrying sensitive electronics (like said hair dryer), you won't need an international adapter that converts the actual voltage.

You'll just need a plug adapter, like this one.

FUN FACT! Nguyen is the most common family name in Vietnam.

✸Hey! Do you know how many girls live their whole lives and never even leave their own country?

Look at you go! You're special. Don't forget that.

INTRODUCTION TO VIETNAM

The Mini Vietnam Bucket List

TOP 10 PLACES TO STAY IN VIETNAM

 01 Floating Airbnb, Lan Ha Bay

02 Vincent's House, Hoi An Ancient City (sometimes known as Vinci Villas)

 03 The Happy Bird B&B, Hoi An Beach

04 Funny Monkeys Homestay, Phong Nha

05 Tam Coc Horizon Bungalow, Ninh Binh

06 Ocean House An Bang, Hoi An Beach

 07 Bac Ha Homestay, Sapa

08 IRINI Boutique Homestay, Mui Ne

 09 Dalat Backpacker's Alley Hostel

10 La Siesta Premium Sai Gon, Ho Chi Minh City

TOP 5 THINGS TO DO IN VIETNAM

01 Ride the Ha Giang Loop (4-days / 3-nights), start in Hanoi ...page 96

02 Vietnamese War Remnants Museum, Ho Chi Minh City...page 265

03 Wander Hoi An Night Market...page 190

04 Cave Camping in Phong Nha ...page 146

05 Travel the country via hop-on / hop-off bus ...page 31

TOP 10 TOURS TO JOIN

 01 Ride the Ha Giang Loop, start in Hanoi

 Ps. Check out my Instagram Highlight about this tour!

 LIFE-CHANGER!

02 Local Food and Beer Tour, Hanoi

 03 Hanoi Food Tour Led by Women on Scooters

04 Street Food Walking Tour, Ho Chi Minh

05 Hoi An Hidden Gems for Early Risers, Hoi An

06 Hoi An Eco Cooking Class

 07 Secret Cocktail Experience, Hoi An

08 Kayaking Lan Ha & Halong Bay

 09 Hai Van Pass Scooter Adventure

10 Mekong Delta Family Homestay

INTRODUCTION TO VIETNAM

The Mini Food & Drink Bucket List

Drink Each Of The Following Once... (✓ Tick as you go!)
- ◯ Bia Hoi (Fresh Beer)
- ◯ Saigon Beer
- ◯ Hanoi Beer
- ◯ Ca Phe (Vietnamese Coffee)
- ◯ Fresh Coconut Water from a Coconut

Eat Each Of The Following Once...
- ◯ Pho (Vietnamese Noodle Soup)
- ◯ Banh Mi (Vietnamese Baguette Sandwich)
- ◯ Banh Xeo (Vietnamese Savory Pancake)
- ◯ Bun Cha (Grilled Pork with Noodles)
- ◯ Com Tam (Broken Rice)
- ◯ Fresh Spring Rolls

✎ **MY FAVORITE THINGS I TRIED AND TASTED IN VIETNAM:**

....

....

....

....

29

HOW TO EXPLORE
THE BEST OF
Vietnam

Ideally, you'd spend three months in Vietnam, slowly eating your way from north to south…

But…30-days is currently (as of 2023) the maximum tourist visa you can get (we'll talk more about visas later).

If you plan it right, 30 days is enough to explore the entirety of the country.

If you're like, "30 days is not possible for me" don't worry. Below I will guide you towards the best adventures for your time budget.

Let's map out some ideal itineraries so that while you read this book, you can easily piece together your plan.

HOW TO EXPLORE VIETNAM

Quick Itineraries

I have traveled up and down Vietnam many times over the years. I've traveled broke, I've traveled luxury - and these itineraries are how I would tell my best friend how to explore this country…including what to see and what to skip.

The Best Way to Explore Vietnam: THE 'HOP ON / HOP OFF BUS

When you buy your Open Bus Ticket package, you'll receive a little notepad of tickets that you can cash in to get you from one-city to another. This is an open bus ticket that allows you to stop in certain towns, stay for as long as you want, and then carry on to the next town when you're ready.

There are multiple packages you can buy that include specific cities, with the option to start in Hanoi or Ho Chi Minh City.

The Full Route Typically looks like this....

❶ **Ho Chi Minh → Mui Ne** = 4.5 Hours

❷ **Mui Ne → Da Lat** = 4 hours

❸ **Da Lat → Nha Trang** = 3.5 hours

❹ **Nha Trang → Hoi An** = 10 hours (overnight sleeper bus)

❺ **Hoi An → Hue** = 3 hours

❻ **Hue → Hanoi** = 14 hours (overnight sleeper bus)

Let's say you get to Mui Ne. Stay for a few days and then decide, "Tomorrow, I'm ready to head to my next destination." Bring your ticket to hotel reception, they'll call the bus station, book you a seat, and you're off.

The two most popular companies are **Viet Nhat and Hanh Cafe**. Expect to pay anywhere from 900k VND to 1,230,000 VND.

The Benefits:

→1 Flat Fee

→The cheapest travel option

Discounted price on busses

→Utterly convenient

→Trusted Bus Company

→Easy way to cover the must-see destinations

→Removes the stress and headache of planning

The Annoyances:

→ Most backpackers buy this ticket, so expect to see the same people. On the bus. In the next town. At your popular hostel. You're all kind of moving at the same pace. This is great if you like them...annoying if you don't.

→ Sleeper buses can get old after you've spent 25 hours laying there – bring entertainment and sleeping pills.

Ps. Avoid Moon Travel (Nguyen Tri Phuong) Tour Bus Company. They've got a bad reputation round' these parts.

Where to book the bus?

At any hostel or travel agency, or here:

The Second Best Way to Explore Vietnam: FOLLOW MY PATH

Want the full Vietnam experience? If you have over three weeks in Vietnam, take the bus, trains, planes and mini-vans to hit up my favorite cities like this…

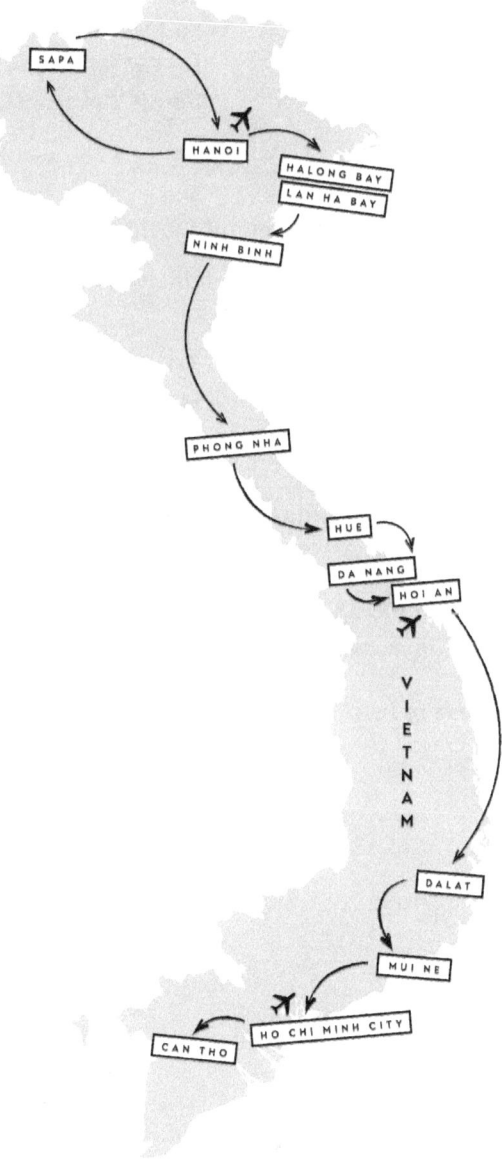

✴ **Travel from the North to the South or South to North**
- and these are the cities that should be on your radar...

→ Hanoi	→ Hoi An Ancient City
→ Ha Giang or Sapa	→ Hoi An Beach
→ Lan Ha or Ha Long Bay	→ Danang
→ Ninh Binh	→ Dalat
→ Phong Nha	→ Mui Ne
→ Hue	→ Ho Chi Minh City
→ Dalat	→ South Vietnam (Can Tho)

....

✴ **Want to move less and absorb more? Do this...**

Travel from the North to the South or South to North like this...

→ Fly into Hanoi	→ Take a bus to Hoi An City
→ Ride the Ha Giang Loop	→ Move to Hoi An Beach
→ Visit Lan Ha Bay	→ Spend one night in Danang
→ Travel to Ninh Binh	→ Fly to Ho Chi Minh City
→ Take an overnight bus to Phong Nha	

(3-weeks to a month)

....

✴ **Have two weeks or less?**

Explore central Vietnam + the north or the south.

Want me to plan your trip for you or want trip-planning advice?
Visit me here at Alexa-West.com

HOW TO EXPLORE VIETNAM

Transportation in Vietnam

How to Get Around

Vietnam is so unique as a backpacker destination in that there is no central hub. Thailand has Bangkok, Cambodia has Phnom Penh, and Malaysia has Kuala Lumpur. But with Vietnam...this S-shaped country has 2 main hubs at opposite ends of the country with bonus destinations spread out north-to-south within a distance of 1,650 kilometers. So, when it comes to covering ground, let's explore your options.

OPTION 1: BUS

Traveling by bus is extremely convenient, especially when it's a sleeper bus. We've already covered the Hop-On / Hop-Off Bus above, but you can also just book buses as you go via your hotel or nearby hostel.

OPTION 2: FLY

If you've got the budget, flying is such a convenient way to get around Vietnam. While the bus from Ho Chi Minh to Nha Trang is 10.5 hours...the plane is only 1 hour. Flying is a great option to cover the country quickly but expect to pair this mode of transport with a couple trains and buses here and there.

The Benefits

✓ Fast

✓ Convenient

✓ Comfortable

The Annoyances

✗ More expensive

✗ Consider transportation costs to and from the airport

✗ Some of the best off-the-beaten path areas have no airport

OPTION 3: TRAIN

The train is one of the most comfortable ways to travel Vietnam! There is always a bathroom, the sleeper trains are comfy, and the train takes some seriously scenic routes.

The Benefits

✓ More leg room

✓ Comfortable for long distances

✓ Available for most destinations

The Annoyances

✗ Less trains per day than buses and planes

✗ Train stations are sometimes a few kilometers away from your final destination town/city

OPTION 4: MOTORBIKE

Driving the length of Vietnam via motorbike is a lifetime bucket list adventure. The memories you make, the people you meet, and the motorbike gang you collect along the way is a once in a lifetime experience...if you are confident on a motorbike.

The Benefits

✓ Get off-the-beaten path with scenic highways and isolated villages

✓ You have instant access to the "Real Vietnam" with detours that other travelers will never get to see

✓ Link up with other motorbike drivers along the way

✓ Train stations are sometimes a few kilometers away from your final destination town/city

The Annoyances

✗ Rainy Weather, Hot Weather, Sweaty Weather

✗ Your ass will get numb and some days will be long

✗ You'll need a Vietnamese or International Drivers License

✗ Motorbikes come with a level of danger and risk – absolutely do not ride without travel insurance

✗ Your bike will break down and you will have to get it fixed along the way – it's just a fact of life that makes the adventure a bit more fun and spontaneous.

Plan to spend at least 5 weeks driving from Ho Chi Minh City to Hanoi. Alternatively, you can always rent a bike and just drive scenic areas for a few days such as the Ha Giang Loop up north.

To get your hands on a motorbike, you'll buy one in Ho Chi Minh and sell it in Hanoi (or the other way around).

PRO TIP! Bring a cup of noodles (there's free hot water on most trains), snacks, and a lot of water for your journey. There will be a snack car but with rip-off prices.

 WHERE TO BUY A BIKE

→ In Ho Chi Minh, head to the neighborhood of Pham Ngu Lao, where there will be countless people trying to sell you a bike. Compare prices and quality. You're essentially choosing a boyfriend, so consider all variables here.

→ The Facebook Group 'Vietnam Backpackers Travel and Sales'

→ A Backpacker Finishing a Trip: Ask around in your hostel or look for signs that resemble 'Missing Cat' posters posted around the backpacker area. You can buy it directly from a backpacker.

Ps. Every single bike must come with a blue registration card – don't buy without one.

The Best Manual Bike for this trip: Honda Win (around $175 depending on condition)

The Best Automatic Bike for this trip: Any automatic scooter -but make sure it has good brakes and decent kick for those uphill mountain roads (around $300 depending on condition).

PRO TIP! If you're unsure about 5 weeks on the road, then come on over to Vietnam, rent a motorbike for a few days and see how it feels. THEN make a decision because girl, once you commit to this wild and crazy adventure, you've really got to commit. It takes a badass.

PRO TIP 2! There are more factors to consider when planning this trip like clothing, food, gasoline- do some deep dive research, first.

You'll find plenty of blogs with bike tips and suggested routes that make this experience so much fucking fun.

OPTION 6: TAXIS AND GRABTAXI

Taxis are widely available in cities and larger towns throughout Vietnam. Companies like Mai Linh and Vinasun are reputable taxi providers with reliable service. Make sure to choose licensed taxis with meters and insist on using them to avoid potential scams.

However, I almost always use GrabTaxi car or motorbike to get around the big cities. Note that these services aren't available in smaller towns like Phong Nha.

OPTION 5: MOTORBIKE TAXIS (XE OM)

Motorbike taxis, known as Xe Om, are a popular means of transportation, especially in urban areas like Hanoi and Ho Chi Minh City. They are convenient for short trips and can weave through traffic quickly. Make sure to negotiate the price before the ride and wear a helmet for safety. Xe Om drivers usually wear identifiable vests and you can flag them down… but no guarantee that they'll speak English.

OPTION 6: WALK

Vietnam's cities and towns are often best explored on foot, allowing you to experience the vibrant atmosphere, discover hidden gems, and interact with locals. Many tourist attractions, markets, and restaurants are within walking distance, so put on comfortable shoes and enjoy strolling around.

VIETNAM
Survival Guide

Visas for Vietnam..40

Weather in Vietnam......................................42

Vietnamese Food Guide.............................45

Vietnamese Language Guide.....................49

What To Pack for Vietnam..........................52

How to Budget to Vietnam.........................55

Internet Data & Vietnam.............................58

Crime & Safety in Vietnam.........................59

VIETNAM LESSON #1:

YOU MUST LEARN HOW TO WALK THROUGH TRAFFIC.

The trick is to keep a steady pace - don't stop - this way drivers can measure your pace and drive around you. Watch how the locals do it.

PRO TIP! When crossing a street or intersection, walk next to a local and keep pace with them.

Visas for Vietnam

Two Options for Tourist Visas in Vietnam

OPTION 1: E-VISA (THIS IS WHAT I USE NOW)

Step 1: Apply for your e- visa online before you come. You can choose 30-day visas or 60-day visas.

9 Where:

Option 1: Through the government website - vietnamvisa.govt.vn/apply-online

Option 2: Through a visa agent. I recommend vietnam-evisa.org

What's the difference? An agent handles the task for you and can expedite the process for you. The government website is a DIY process, and slightly cheaper.

Step 2: Fill out the online form.

Step 3: Make your payment for the Visa Approval Letter.

Step 4: Receive your Visa Approval Letter via email and print it out.

Step 5: At the airport or border crossing in Vietnam, present your Visa Approval Letter to the visa counter.

Step 6: Receive your Visa Sticker in your passport (yep, a full-page sticker – not a stamp).

OPTION 2: VISA EXEMPTION:

→ Citizens of certain countries can visit without a visa, aka visa on arrival.

→ Citizens of France, Germany, Italy, Spain, Sweden, the United Kingdom, South Korea, Belarus, Sweden, Norway, Denmark, Finland, Iceland, Japan and Russia, can enter Vietnam without a visa for up to 45 days. For countries like Denmark, Finland, Norway, and Russia, the visa exemption period is extended to 30 days.

→ Double check with CIBTvisas.com to make sure this information is correct as it applies to your citizenship - and if you want to stay longer than 15 days, apply for the E-visa above so that you don't have to do a visa run after 15 days.

SURVIVAL GUIDE

Weather for Vietnam

Unlike its Southeast Asian neighbors, Vietnam's weather cannot be summarized with one simple pattern. Stretching over 3,000 kilometers from North to South, each region offers a distinct environment, ranging from dry deserts to icy mountain passages.

Spoiler: I'm going to tell you the "best times to visit" each region...but understand that it is impossible to visit Vietnam and hit all the "best times" for each region in one visit. Use this weather section to help you pack. Then go no matter what.

Ps. My favorite memories (plural because this has happened more than once) in Vietnam are the times that the streets have flooded and I've walked around the streets with water to my knees, drinking a beer and ducking into restaurants to find other travelers doing the same, laughing. Vietnam is Earth at its finest. Embrace it!

THE FAR NORTH

The "Far North" typically refers to areas beyond Hanoi, including destinations like Sapa and Ha Giang. Here, you can expect colder temperatures and more rainfall. Prepare to layer and bring a light rain jacket.

- ✷ **Hottest Months:** June - August (around 21°C / 70°F) with sporadic heavy rain to provide relief from the heat.
- ✷ **Coldest Months:** December - January (around 10-12°C / 50-54°F) with dry but frosty conditions.
- ✷ **Wettest Months:** June - July with heavy mist and prolonged rain.
- ✷ **Official Monsoon Season:** April - September.
- ✷ **Most Ideal Time to Visit:** February - April (to avoid the coldest and wettest months).

THE NORTH

North Vietnam is home to popular backpacking destinations such as Hanoi, Halong Bay, and Ninh Binh. While you'll generally experience drier and warmer weather compared to the mountains, you're not yet in tropical territory.

Hanoi has two distinct seasons: one resembling Seattle or London with gray skies, rainy days, and cooler temperatures, and the other feeling more like Florida with hot and humid weather.

- **Hottest Months:** September (around 28-29°C / 82-84°F) and wet.
- **Coldest Months:** January - March (around 17-22°C / 63-72°F) and dry.
- **Wettest Months:** July - September.
- **Official Monsoon Season:** May - October.
- **Most Ideal Time to Visit:** August - October for a mix of warm and dry weather.

THE CENTER

In terms of weather, Central Vietnam is a dream come true. Cities like Hoi An, Hue, and Nha Trang enjoy a temperate climate with dry conditions and pleasant tank-top weather throughout much of the year…but there is rain!

- **Hottest Months:** June - August (around 34-35°C / 93-95°F) and dry.
- **Coldest Months:** December - February (around 25-26°C / 77-79°F).
- **Wettest Months:** October - November with heavy but short showers.
- **Official Monsoon Season:** September - December.
- **Most Ideal Time to Visit:** December – May for moderate temperatures.

THE SOUTH

Unlike the northern regions, Southern Vietnam experiences relatively stable weather. Prepare for occasional storms, but overall, this region is an excellent starting or ending point for a trip across Vietnam. Southern destinations include Ho Chi Minh City, Mui Ne, the Mekong Delta, and Phu Quoc Island.

••

✹ **Hottest Months:** March - May (around 29-30°C / 84-86°F) and dry.

✹ **Coldest Months:** October - December (around 27°C / 81°F) with occasional showers.

✹ **Wettest Months:** June - August with short but heavy afternoon showers.

✹ **Official Monsoon Season:** May - November.

✹ **Most Ideal Time to Visit:** December - March for fewer crowds and dry weather.

••

So, here's a helpful tip for planning your Vietnam itinerary:

→ If visiting during Spring/Summer, travel from South to North.

→ If visiting during Autumn/Winter, travel from North to South.

NERVOUS?

Even I get nervous before (and during) a new trip. The secret? Turn that nervous energy into excited energy. Instead of saying "I'm afraid to do this" say "I can't wait to do this" and let life happen.

SURVIVAL GUIDE

Vietnamese Food Guide
BECAUSE TRAVEL IS JUST AN EXCUSE TO EAT, RIGHT?

Okay, for your reading pleasure! Try to pronounce these words. If you can't, that's okay. It's still so helpful to be able to identify them on a menu.

Pork: Teet lone (Thịt lợn)
Beef: Teet baw (Thịt bò)
Chicken: Ga (Gà)
Lamb: Tohm (Tôm)
Shrimp: Teet kew (Thịt cừu)
Fish: Kah (Cá)
Vegetarian: Tee-yeung Vee-yet (Tiếng Việt)

Here is your official Vietnam food & drink bucket list…

Pho: Pronounced 'Fuh', this is the most well-known Vietnamese dish within the Western world. Deep broth with tender chicken, beef, pork, or seafood along with freshly made rice noodles, Pho is the ultimate comfort food. Season to your liking with soy sauce, chili, and lime on the side.

Fried Spring Rolls…Nem Ran (in the North) / Cha Gio (in the South): Crispy deep-fried spring rolls typically filled with pork, shrimp or kept vegetarian. Often served with Bun Cha in the North. They're not always pretty…but they're always delicious.

Fresh Spring Rolls/Goi Cuon: Shrimp, lettuce, vermicelli noodles and cilantro wrapped in rice paper and served with a sweet & sour fish sauce or a peanut dipping sauce.

Banh Cuon: Steamed rice rolls filled with ground pork and wood ear mushrooms, topped with crispy fried shallots and served with a dipping sauce.

Bahn Mi: Vietnamese sandwich made with a crusty baguette filled with various ingredients such as pâté, grilled meats (pork, chicken, or beef), pickled vegetables, cilantro, mayo and chili sauce.

Bun Cha

(BUN CHA 33 CO IN HANOI)

Freshly grilled and perfectly seasoned pork is served in a tangy broth with pickled veggies. With your chopsticks, grab a mouthful of sticky noodles, mint, lettuce and mix together in one bite. Watch the locals around you to figure it out.

Bún Bò Nam Bộ: Not a soup; yet not a salad- Bún bò nam bộ mixes a little bit of everything in one savory bowl. Rice noodles, beef, peanuts, lettuce, crispy dried shallots, and a deep broth collide to create my favorite dish in Vietnam.

Bún Bò Huế

A specialty from the town of Hue, Bun Bo Hue is a bowl of spicy beef noodle soup made with rice vermicelli noodles and seasoned beef patties, garnished with chilies, chopped cilantro and lime…and my absolute favorite Vietnamese dish!

Grilled Shrimp - Tôm Nướng: Whole shrimp grilled on a stick and served with a side of dipping sauce, the trick is to remove the head first and suck out the sweet, creamy brains.

Cao Lau: A specialty of Hoi An, this bowl of pork or beef broth and meat is distinct when it comes to its thick, chewy noodles, fried lard and tangy sauce that you mix all together. Fun fact: There are only two families in Hoi An who make and supply all the Cau Lau noodles.

Go on the "Early Riser" tour to see how they are made.

Xoi Xeo: A sweet sticky rice with mung bean paste, fried shallots, fried egg, stewed pork and shredded pork is about as close to soul food as it gets in Vietnam.

Bánh Xèo

Vietnamese savory pancake made from rice flour, turmeric, and coconut milk that looks more like a taco as it wraps up a mixture of protein, usually shrimp or pork, with crunchy veggies, scallions and tangy sauce.

Broken Rice - Cơm Tấm

Literally, broken pieces of rice, this grain tastes more like couscous. Served as the working-class lunch staple, Com Tam is dished up with your choosing of sides like sweet grilled chicken or sautéed veggies. Look out for Com Tam places on the side of the road with a 'point & choose' display case.

Cha Ca: A Hanoi delicacy, Cha Ca is a dish of grilled fish (typically catfish) marinated in turmeric, served with vermicelli noodles, peanuts, herbs, and shrimp paste.

Hot Pot: Vietnamese love a good Hot Pot; not just for the vibrant flavors but for the social aspect of cooking meat and veggies in one communal simmering pot of broth. When it comes to Hot Pot, you've got option: Vit Nau Chao (Duck hot pot), Lau Hai San (seafood hot pot), Lau Ca Keo (fish hot pot with small fish that look similar to eel), Lau Chua (sweet & sour hot pot with river fish.

FOOD ETIQUETTE TO CONSIDER

✓**Try local street food:** Some of the most authentic and delicious Vietnamese food can be found in street stalls and markets. Embrace the vibrant street food culture, but choose stalls with good hygiene practices.

✓**Use chopsticks:** Learn how to use chopsticks, as they are the primary utensil for most Vietnamese meals.

✓**Sharing is common:** In Vietnamese dining culture, it's common to order multiple dishes and share them with others at the table. This communal style of eating allows you to experience a variety of flavors.

✓**Try the fresh herbs and condiments:** Vietnamese cuisine often incorporates fresh herbs, lettuce, and condiments like chili sauce, fish sauce, and lime that are just placed on the table, free for you to experience and enhance the flavors of your dishes.

✓**Slurping is acceptable:** When enjoying noodles or soup, it is acceptable to slurp your food as it shows appreciation and enjoyment.

DRINKS

Street Beer - Bia Hoi: Homemade street beer that is typically served out of family run establishments or just a keg on the side of the road, this beer is sold for as low as 4,000 dong and has a slight buttery taste to it.

Sugar Cane Juice- Nước Mía: No refined sugar here, just pure organic sugar cane juice full of electrolytes. You'll see little stands on the side of the road with fresh sugar cane juice that is crushed as it's run through a machine, with its pure juice poured over ice.

Iced Black Coffee – Ca Fe Da: Strong drip coffee, black. But make a point to ask for no sugar.

Sweetened Iced Coffee- Ca Fe Sua Da: The most popular style of coffee in Vietnam is this iced coffee that is sweetened with condensed milk, creating a thick, slow-drinking treat.

Coconut Coffee - Cà Phê Dừa: Instead of milk or sweetened cream, add coconut cream to your iced coffee for an exotic texture and flavor.

Egg Coffee - Cà Phê Trứng: For ages, when I heard "Egg Coffee" I imagined a raw egg being dropped into a cup of coffee – but I was so wrong. Egg Coffee is a sweet whipped cream made of egg and sugar that is added into a black coffee to make a thick and tasty coffee that resembles a dense latte.

SURVIVAL GUIDE

Vietnamese Language Guide

...I'm not even going to waste space in this book by giving you an entire language guide filled with words that you need to hear in order to pronounce. Instead, we will cover the simple basics.

With 6 different tones and dozens of dialects, Vietnamese is considered one of the most difficult languages in the world so what you really need is a tutorial where you can listen, practice and repeat.

Start with this video ☞

And then circle back to these basic phrases.

NUMBERS

One	Một (Muht)
Two	Hai (High)
Three	Ba (Bah)
Four	Bốn (Bawn)
Five	Năm (Nahm)
Six	Sáu (Sow)
Seven	Bảy (By)
Eight	Tám (Tahm)
Nine	Chín (Cheen)
Ten	Mười (Moo-ee)

Eleven	Mười một (Moo-ee muht)
Twenty	Hai mươi (High moo-ee)
Thirty	Ba mươi (Bah moo-ee)
Forty	Bốn mươi (Bawn moo-ee)
Fifty	Năm mươi (Nahm moo-ee)
Sixty	Sáu mươi (Sow moo-ee)
Seventy	Bảy mươi (By moo-ee)
Eighty	Tám mươi (Tahm moo-ee)
Ninety	Chín mươi (Cheen moo-ee)
One Hundred	Một trăm (Muht trahm)
One Hundred Ten	Một trăm mười (Muht trahm moo-ee)

DAY-TO-DAY VOCABULARY

Hello	Xin chào (Sin chow)
Thank You	Cám ơn (Kahm uhn)
Yes	Vâng (Vahng)
No	Không (Khom)
Please	Làm ơn (Lahm uhn)
Excuse Me / Sorry	Xin lỗi (Sin loy)
Good-Bye	Tạm biệt (Tahm byet)
How Are You?	Bạn khỏe không? (Bahn khwe khom?)
I'm Fine, Thank You	Tôi khỏe, cám ơn (Toy khwe, kahm uhn)
What Is Your Name?	Bạn tên là gì? (Bahn ten lah zee?)
My Name Is….	Tên tôi là… (Ten toy lah…)

Where Is…?	…ở đâu? (…uh dow?)
How Much Is This?	Cái này bao nhiêu tiền? (Kai nay bah-woe nyew tyen?)
I Don't Understand	Tôi không hiểu (Toy khom hyew)
Help!	Giúp đỡ! (Yoop daw!)
I Want…	Tôi muốn… (Toy mwohn…)
Where Is The Bathroom?	Nhà vệ sinh ở đâu? (Nyah veh sinh uh dow?)
Delicious	Ngon (Ngon)
Cheers!	Chúc mừng (Chook moong)

I also recommend that you begin to learn via language learning apps like Duolingo or HelloTalk.

✎ TRAVEL NOTES:

....

....

....

....

....

SURVIVAL GUIDE

What to Pack for Vietnam

I help you pack for Vietnam in depth on my website and travel shop - but, here's an overview of what to expect:

Passport with at Least 6 Months Validity: Ensure that your passport is valid for at least six months from your entry date to Vietnam.

WHAT TO PACK

THE PERFECT BACKPACK

Backpack or Suitcase

Opt for a backpack rather than a rolling suitcase, as Vietnam's sidewalks and transportation options may not be suitcase-friendly. A backpack is more convenient, especially if you plan to explore different regions or go on adventures like hiking or motorbike trips.

The Bag I Recommend…The Osprey Farpoint 40 Backpack.

It's been over 5 years that I've been using this bag. I love it so much that I just bought the exact same model again to use for another 5 years.

Or the Osprey Fairview 55 that comes with a zip-on and off day bag. This bag is technically not carry-on size, but I haven't been stopped for it, so far. The key is not overstuffing the bag. Keep it looking slim. If you have heavy stuff, put it in the day bag and zip it off as your "personal item".

TRAVEL INSURANCE

It is highly recommended to have travel insurance that covers medical emergencies, trip cancellations, and other unforeseen circumstances. Research and choose a reputable travel insurance provider that offers coverage in Vietnam.

BACKPACK OR SUITCASE

Opt for a backpack rather than a rolling suitcase, as Vietnam's sidewalks and transportation options may not be suitcase-friendly. A backpack is more convenient, especially if you plan to explore different regions or go on adventures like hiking or motorbike trips.

COMFORTABLE WALKING SHOES

Vietnam involves a lot of walking and exploring, so it's essential to have comfortable footwear. Pack a sturdy pair of walking shoes or sneakers that can handle various terrains.

LIGHTWEIGHT CLOTHING

Vietnam has a tropical climate, so pack lightweight, breathable clothing suitable for hot and humid weather. Include items like shorts, t-shirts, lightweight pants or skirts, and dresses. It's also a good idea to bring a light jacket or sweater for cooler evenings, especially in the north.

RAIN GEAR

Vietnam experiences rainy seasons in certain regions, so it's wise to pack a compact raincoat or travel umbrella to stay dry during unexpected showers.

TRAVEL ADAPTER

Vietnam typically uses Type A, Type C, and Type F electrical outlets, so bring a universal travel adapter to charge your electronic devices.

INSECT REPELLENT

Protect yourself from mosquito bites by packing insect repellent.

SUNSCREEN AND HAT

Vietnam can have strong sun exposure, so pack sunscreen with a high SPF to protect your skin. Additionally, bring a hat or a cap for extra sun protection.

CASH AND BANK CARDS

While Vietnam is becoming more card-friendly, you'll want to carry some cash in Vietnamese Dong for smaller establishments and local markets. Bring at least two bank cards (debit and/or credit) for emergencies and ensure they are from different providers to have backup options if one card malfunctions or gets lost.

EMPTY SPACE IN YOUR BAG

Leave some extra space in your bag for souvenirs and shopping during your trip. Vietnam offers various unique crafts, clothing, and goods that you may want to bring back home.

WHAT NOT TO PACK
✗ Jeans
✗ High-heels
✗ Hairspray (ya won't use it)
✗ A Curling Iron (with this humidity...no point)
✗ Too Many Bras (ya won't wear em')
✗ A Pharmacy of Medicine (you can get it all here)

SHOP MY TRAVEL ESSENTIALS...

If it's on Amazon, it will be in my Amazon Storefront here:

SURVIVAL GUIDE

How to Budget for Vietnam

What is the least amount I can spend and still see it all?

If you are on a tight budget, you can aim for a daily budget of around $30 to $40. Stay in budget accommodations like hostels or guesthouses, eat at local street food stalls and small local restaurants, use public transportation or shared taxis, and focus on free or low-cost activities such as exploring markets, visiting temples, and enjoying nature.

DAILY EXPENSES (PRICES IN USD)

Street Food	$1 - $3
Local Restaurant	$3 - $8
Western-Style Restaurant	$8 - $15
Bottle of Beer	$1-$2
Cocktail	$3-$7
Hostel Dorm Bed	$5-$15
Mid-Range Hotel	$30-$70
Upscale Hotel or Resort	$80
Day Tour	$10-$50
Domestic Flight	$30-$110
Long-Distance Bus	$10-$30

TIPS TO SPEND LESS IN VIETNAM:

💰 Eat local street food: Street food in Vietnam is not only delicious but also affordable. Try local specialties like pho, banh mi, and banh xeo from street vendors.

💰 Bargain at markets: When shopping at markets or dealing with street vendors, don't be afraid to negotiate for a better price. Start with a lower offer and work your way up.

💰 Use public transportation: Utilize local buses, trains, or shared taxis instead of private taxis or tourist transportation services to save money on transportation.

💰 Explore free attractions: Vietnam has numerous attractions that are free or have a minimal entrance fee. Take advantage of these to save on admission costs.

💰 Travel during the shoulder or low season: Accommodation and flight prices tend to be cheaper during shoulder seasons or the low season. Consider traveling during these periods to save money.

💰 Avoid unnecessary expenses: Be mindful of your spending on alcohol, nightlife, and organized tours. These can quickly add up and significantly impact your budget.

HOW TO USE MONEY IN VIETNAM

Vietnamese currency is called the **Vietnamese Dong (VND)**. Cash is widely used in Vietnam, especially for street food, transportation, and smaller establishments. Here are some tips to help you manage your money in Vietnam...

❶ **Familiarize Yourself with Vietnamese Dong:**

The Vietnamese Dong comes in various denominations, so it's important to become familiar with the different bill and coin values. Here are the commonly used banknote denominations:

💴 500,000 VND (yellow)

💴 200,000 VND (light brown)

💴 100,000 VND (blue)

💴 50,000 VND (pink/purple)

💴 20,000 VND (green)

💴 10,000 VND (red)

❷ How much cash to bring to Vietnam:

I always recommend bringing around $100-$300 USD in emergency cash to exchange only if necessary. Instead, plan to use your debit card to withdraw cash in Vietnamese Dong from ATMs.

❸ Cards You Should Be Traveling With:

☞ **Travel Credit Card:** Using a travel credit card can be beneficial for booking flights, hotels, and larger purchases. It offers protection and often provides travel rewards or points.

☞ **Debit Card:** Consider getting a debit card with no foreign transaction fees. I travel with the debit card from Charles Schwab Bank, which does not charge you any transaction fees and reimburses you for any fees a foreign ATM fees abroad.

❹ Currency Conversion Trick:

Don't get ripped off. Know how much you're spending with a currency cheat sheet.

On a piece of paper, write down each Vietnamese note and its rough equivalent in your currency. For example:

→ 50k = ~$2 USD

→ 100k = ~ 4 USD

…write it all down on a piece of paper and take a picture. Save that picture as your wallpaper. Now, whenever you're in a market and want to haggle or know the price of something quickly, you just have to glance at your phone to do the conversion.

SURVIVAL GUIDE

Internet & Data in Vietnam

Get a SIM Card Immediately. Internet access will be your lifeline…and only for $13.

In Vietnam especially, you'll find that you heavily rely on a SIM card for necessary internet shenanigans like…

- → Google Maps
- → Getting un-lost
- → Tinder (yea…why not?)
- → Life in General

When you land at the airport, after you pass through customs and enter the arrival hall, you'll see plenty of kiosks selling SIM Cards.

Look for the carrier Mobifone or Viettel. A 4G plan with UNLIMITED Data for 1 month is around $9 USD/ 200k VND. You'll have package options that include phone calls, which I've found useful. But it's not a must.

The customer service dude will set everything up for you. Just check that your mobile data is working before you leave the kiosk.

I made a video tutorial of this process on Instagram here:

If you enter Vietnam by land or forget to buy a Sim at the airport, find one of these stores in town for the most comprehensive data packages and staff that will set everything up for you:

▢ **Viettel Store / Mobifone Store / TheGioidiDong**

SURVIVAL GUIDE

Crime & Safety in Vietnam

The scams, the tricks, the dangers – and how to avoid them all…

Rule of Thumb: Vietnam gets safer and safer the further north you travel

The most crime-ridden city is Ho Chi Minh. The biggest crime? Street theft. Watch your pockets, wear a cross shoulder purse, and don't leave your purse or phone out in the open. Besides pickpockets, here's what else you need to know…

LEARN HOW TO CROSS THE STREET

Crossing the street in Vietnam is a skill. One you must master. Stop lights are sparse and even when they are present, they aren't always obeyed. So, you must learn to be one with the traffic!

You'll notice quickly that when driving, motorbikes will weave around each other in an organized form of chaos. This chaos means that you can't predict their path. Instead, let the motorbikes predict yours.

You'll cross the street in 2 phases, pausing in the middle of the road.

Wait until you see a slight pocket in the traffic and keep your eyes on the bikes while walking at a steady pace to the middle of the road. Then repeat while watching the other direction. All the while, be aware of rogue drivers that may be driving the wrong way on the side that you're not watching.

Do not stop or jump or jerk or run. Walk at a consistent pace so bikes can move around you.

To get the hang of this, simply wait for a local to cross the street and follow their lead.

MOTORBIKES AND CAR CRASHES

Man oh man. There are far too many traffic accidents in Vietnam. You have monster 16-wheel trucks next to tiny motorbikes passing each other on dirt roads. You have cows on the road. You have drunk drivers galore.

♥ Where: Particularly in Hanoi and Ho Chi Minh city.

What to do: Always wear your seatbelt in a car and always secure your helmet tightly when riding a motorbike. Don't ride or drive with someone you have an uneasy feeling about. Practice riding your motorbike in rural areas before driving in the city or on main roads.

DONUT LADIES

Don't trust their "free donut" gimmick. In the big cities, women walk around carrying baskets of fried bread. They'll entice you to try one "for free", but once you take a bite, they will not leave you alone until you buy. They might follow you or physically grab you until you buy. And watch for the 'swapping your 500k note for a 50k note' trick. These ladies are masters at getting the most out of naive tourists.

Do's & Dont's for Vietnam

Beyond crime, there are a couple social and cultural things that you need to know before you go.

DO...

✓ Carry Small Notes

Most places can't break a 500k bill. It's best to break these in a restaurant or convenient store ASAP.

✓ Carry a Shawl

You'll need to cover your shoulders anytime you enter a pagoda or a Buddhist Temple. Also, those bus rides get cold! You can use your shawl as a blanket.

✓ Carry Toilet Paper

Most toilets don't have toilet paper. BUT at nearly every shop, you can find little rectangular packets of tissue that will fit in your purse. You'll need these as most toilets just have a 'bum gun' used like a bidet.

✓ Dress like You're on Vacation with your Parents

Keep your beach wear on the beach tasteful when it comes to short shorts and low-cut tops. Boobies and butt cheeks should be modest. Oh, and don't bicycle around town in a bikini top. Police have actually started fining tourists for this in some towns.

✓ Remember to Drink Lots of Water

It's easy to forget! The heat (and beer) will dehydrate you so quickly in Vietnam. Don't neglect that refreshing H2O.

✓ Have Travel Insurance

Motorbike crashes are common here, crossing the road is sketchy, and all outdoor activities come with risk. Luckily, Vietnam has a fabulous international health care system. You'd be a silly girl not to travel with travel insurance.

My go-to for travel insurance is WorldNomads.com and Safetywing.com. They'll both cover everything from doctor visits for a tummy ache and medivacs in case you fall off a mountain (that shit happens).

✓ Negotiate Prices

In markets or when dealing with street vendors, bargaining is common in Vietnam. Don't be afraid to negotiate prices, but do so respectfully and with a smile. It can be a fun and engaging experience, but remember to be fair to the sellers as well.

DON'T...

✗ Don't Disrespect Ho Chi Minh

Ho Chi Minh, the revered leader of Vietnam's independence movement, holds a special place in Vietnamese hearts. It is important not to speak disrespectfully about him or display any form of disrespect towards his image or statues.

✗ Don't Show Off

You want to look like you have no money and nothing to steal. Keep your phone, iPad, and laptop low key.

✗ Don't Volunteer Short-Term

Any volunteer program that involves an orphanage or a 1-4-week stint teaching English to children is a scam and exploits Vietnamese youth. If you want to volunteer, be ready to commit to at least 3 months.

✗ Don't Cause Vietnamese People to "Lose Face"

Vietnamese people do not take embarrassment or confrontation lightly. Causing a fuss, losing your temper or disrespecting a local can put you in some serious danger. Smile through even the bitchiest interactions and you're more likely to get your way.

✗ Don't Take Pictures or Videos without Permission

Uniformed police officers eating an ice cream cone, Vietnamese women wearing traditional dresses, and especially children in villages – always ask permission before you take someone's picture.

✗ Don't Talk about the Vietnam War

If a local elder engages you in wartime conversation, the safest bet is just not to get into it. However, these conversations can be more open-minded and insightful with college-aged Vietnamese. This young generation of Vietnamese are incredibly insightful.

✗ Don't Show Public Affection

While holding hands is generally acceptable in Vietnam, avoid excessive public displays of affection, especially in more conservative areas. Save intimate moments for private spaces out of respect for local culture and customs.

✗ Don't Drink Tap Water

Similar to many countries around the globe, it's advisable to avoid drinking tap water in Vietnam. Stick to bottled water, which is readily available and affordable. However, you can brush your teeth with the tap water and shower in it with no worries.

Now! No more stressing. You've got all the information you need to travel safely. You can handle this.

Tell your anxiety to piss off and let's plan your trip to Vietnam!

Ps. GoogleMaps is your friend in this country. I've removed most of the addresses in this book because…GoogleMaps. Just type in the name and you're on your way.

☆ Journal Moment ☆

Now that you have an idea of how to spend your time, let's take a moment to set your intention for your trip to Vietnam Your intention can be just to have fun and explore, or to spend some quality time with yourself. Maybe your intention is to heal. Or to step outside of your confort zone.

Whatever intention you set, it will set the tone of your trip and call out to the right people and situations aligned with it.

Big magic will unfold, you'll see.

✎ **MY INTENTION FOR THIS TRIP TO VIETNAM IS...**

....

....

....

....

....

....

And now...let's discover Vietnam ♥

CHAPTER ONE

Hanoi

DAYS NEEDED:

3 days/4 nights

BEST FOR:

Lots of history, sipping coffees in the morning and going on food tours at night.

CHAPTER ONE

Hanoi

Hanoi is chapter one because it's my #1 must-see destination, and I'm going to show you why.

The capital of Vietnam and the former communist headquarters during the Vietnam war is Hanoi, a beautiful juxtaposition of old vs. new.

Most of this city isn't trying to be anything that it's not. Life here moves at a slow pace for such a big city. The neighborhoods seem quite content with their old school buildings that crumble away, revealing red bricks and years of layered paint and graffiti. The locals are chill in the way that they have kept the same morning coffee routine for 40 years and kids still play soccer in the streets at night. There's always a winding alley to get lost in, street food to be had, temples to be explored, and locals offering you some fresh Bia Hoi.

Then, scattered amongst the old Hanoi, you'll find pockets of expat areas with shiny hotels and western food and spas with gelish pedicures. You get a little bit of everything in Hanoi.

With a history spanning over a thousand years, Hanoi showcases a fascinating mix of traditional Vietnamese culture and French colonial influence. The Old Quarter, known as "36 Streets," is the heart of Hanoi and is a maze of narrow streets filled with shops, cafes, and historical sites and food. One of the highlights of Hanoi is its food scene! From street food stalls to elegant restaurants, the city is a paradise for food lovers and food tours. While you're here, you must try the local specialty, cha ca, a sizzling fish dish like you've never had.

Hanoi also serves as a gateway to my must-do adventures in Vietnam: the Ha Giang Loop and Ninh Binh. A trip to Vietnam without a visit to Hanoi should be illegal.

LIFE-CHANGER!

FUN FACT! I lived in Hanoi by myself for three months. It is extremely safe.

CHAPTER 1: HANOI

Areas to Explore in Hanoi

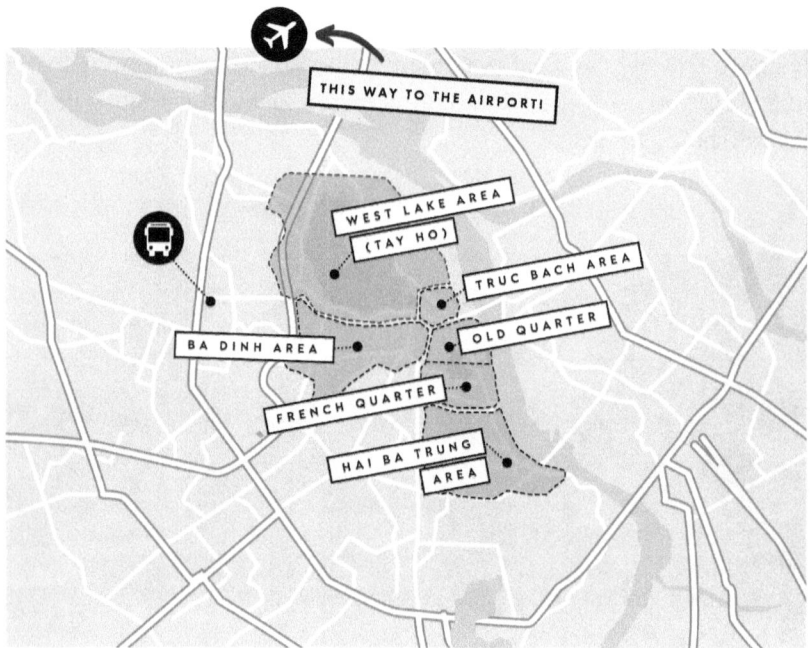

OLD QUARTER

All the fast-paced action happens in the Old Quarter. It's a shopping dream, a party paradise and a foodie heaven. There are hotels, bars, and stores for all ages, price ranges, and purposes. You could easily stay in the Old Quarter for your whole vacay while still seeing the nearby temples and sights. Be sure to visit the areas of Ta Hien Beer Street not just at night, but also in the early mornings where locals sit on plastic stools sipping coffee.

HOAN KIEM LAKE

Starting at the south end of the Old Quarter, Hoan Kiem Lake is a great place to wander during the day and night. Home to little islands with ancient pagodas, parks with beer vendors, and Hanoi's only McDonalds on the south end, Haon Kiem has a fun perimeter to wander. There are tons of upscale hotels in this area with nice restaurants to go along with them.

TAY HO & TRUC BACH

These expat areas are low-key and picturesque versions of a bustling city. Tons of western food, lots of little parks, lake views, and western amenities. Get your laptop, find a café, and blend in with the expats.

BA DINH (MY OLD HOOD)

I used to live here. This is a neighborhood that doesn't see too many foreigners. You can get lost in back alleys where you'll stumble upon a quaint coffee shop, a local pho spot or a school supplies store with cheap notepads and pens galore! This area is very local but still very approachable. I'll be listing some of my favorite places to eat and drink within this neighborhood in this book. To get here, just take a quick GrabTaxi or walk along the lake.

FUN FACT! Hanoi measns "City of Lakes" because it's built on the banks of the Red River and so many rivers still flow around and through the city, forming lakes like Thein Quang Lake, Hoan Kien Lake, Truk Bach Lake, Bay Mau Lake and Tu Le Lake.

CHAPTER 1: HANOI

Where to Stay in Hanoi

LA SINFONÍA DEL REY HOTEL & SPA

Location doesn't get any better than this! Located right next to the main round-about at the top of Hoan Kiem Lake, you're near all the western food, the upscale Vietnamese food, the best happy hours, and literally on the edge of Old Quarter. At night, the park around the lake comes alive with street food and entertainers. When you're all tuckered out, crawl back into your dreamy bed with chic design and maybe have a nightcap on your private balcony or at the rooftop bar. This place is beyond perfect for a solo girl.

Budget: $$$
Where: Hoan Kiem Lake

Book Here:

HANOI PAON HOTEL & SPA

Hanoi gets hot in the spring and summer. Really hot. After a day of wandering the sweaty city, sometimes all you want is a pool. The rooftop pool at Hanoi Paon Hotel will do the trick. There's not much in terms of lounge chairs but throw a towel down and you've got the perfect tanning spot. Plus, the glittering view of the city at night is gorgeous. Located right in Old Quarter with cozy beds, free breakfast, and friendly reception, this place is a steal.

Budget: $$
Where: Old Quarter

Book Here:

HÔTEL DU LAC HANOI

Hear me out. After a trip up to Sapa or Ha Giang when it's cold or when you've been on the back of a motorbike for three days, all you will want to do is return to Hanoi and take a hot bath. Then crawl upstairs to the rooftop bar and have a cocktail with panoramic views of the city. Rest your feet, absorb the atmosphere and melt into one of the best beds in Vietnam.

Budget: $$$
Where: Hoan Kiem Lake   Book Here:

SPLENDID HOLIDAY HOTEL

Spring for the Junior Suite with Balcony! This is an affordable gem tucked right in the heart of enchanting Hanoi! You'll be swooning over the breathtaking views of St. Joseph's Cathedral and the easy access to all the amazing cultural spots in the city. The rooftop terrace is an absolute dream! Picture yourself unwinding with a cup of coffee, gazing at the mesmerizing cityscape – pure bliss! And let me tell you, the on-site restaurant serves up some seriously delicious Vietnamese delicacies that will have your taste buds doing a happy dance. This place is an absolute must for a fantastic and unforgettable stay in Hanoi that doesn't break the bank!

Budget: $$
Where: In the Old Quarter   Book Here:

MAYA BOUTIQUE HOTEL

My second pick for a private room on a budget (besides Splendid Holiday Hotel). I typically stay at Maya Boutique Hotel, where you're close enough to Hanoi life that you wake up with the sound of motorbikes and shops opening, but far enough that you don't hear too much of the party. These are clean rooms with lovely staff and private bathrooms within walking distance to everything in Old Quarter.

Budget: $
Where: In the Old Quarter   Book Here:

HANOI BUFFALO HOSTEL

The best location possible is this chill hostel in the heart of Hanoi. It's clean, it's safe, the vibes are social but not too crazy and you've got the best exploring right outside your door. Plus, staying here saves you money. You get free breakfast, a free walking tour of the city, free beer at 7pm, and a free bar crawl at 10pm. Stay in an all-female dorm, mixed dorm or a private room.

Budget: $
Where: In the Old Quarter

Book Here:

FUN FACT! The Long Bien bridge was designed by Gustave Eiffel. Yep, the same man who designed the Eiffel Tower in Paris and the Statue of Liberty.

CHAPTER 1: HANOI

Where to Stay in Hanoi

COFFEE & CAFES IN HANOI

Hanoi has the best coffee culture in the world. Not only is the coffee strong and flavorful but the cafes are so mysterious and full of character. Upon arrival, straight-up Google "hidden cafes" for some of the best spots. Sometimes you'll find a coffee vendor down a discrete alleyway or in the courtyards of someone's house.

Coffee in Hanoi is often served with milk - but the super sweet condensed milk. This means that the coffee is very thick and rich with a unique flavor.

If you want your cup a bit more specialized, check out these cafes below…

HIDDEN GEM COFFEE

Walk through a narrow yellow alleyway and enter into a hidden world of bright yellow walls, red lanterns and lush greenery. Hidden Gem Coffee is truly an oasis in the city. They've got the classic coffees but they've also got smoothies and teas to help jump start your day. Try the fruit spring rolls for a quirky take on breakfast.

☉ **Open:** Daily 8am-10pm
♀ **Where:** Old Quarter
🚇 **Address:** 3b P. Hàng Tre, Lý Thái Tổ
♥ @hiddengemcoffeehanoi

HANOI 1990'S TRAINSTREET

…people will tell you that train street isn't running anymore but they're wrong! Head to this little cafe situated on the sides of the train tracks and order a coconut coffee. Then, tuck your knees in and watch your toes as the train tightly squeezes through this small street lined with cafes and homes!

I made an Instagram reel on this experience here:

Oh and here are the train times as per this very official sign posted at the train tracks. But hey, this is Vietnam and sometimes the trains are late. It's not a problem as long as you have a good drink in your hand.

9:00 am	14:25 pm
5:20 am	15:45 pm
6:00 am	19:10 pm
10:00 am	19:30 pm
12:25 pm	20:00 pm

☉ **Open:** Daily 8am-9pm
♥ **Where:** 6-minute drive from Old Quarter
🚇 **Address:** Ngõ 222 Đ. Lê Duẩn, Khâm Thiên

HOON CAFE

I only know about this hidden local cafe because I used to live in this hidden local restaurant. HOON Cafe is not used to seeing tourists - but in a good way. This tiny shoebox cafe is tucked way in a side street, where cool young people come to grab a coffee with their friends in between classes or work. There's a couch inside and some chairs outside in the courtyard. They only take cash and smiles. **PRO TIP!** Come here before or after Bun Cha 33 Co which I write about below. They are walking distance to each other.

☉ **Open:** Daily 9am-6pm
♥ **Where:** Ba Dinh – South of West Lake
🚇 **Address:** 40/267 Hoang Hoa Tham str
♥ @hoon.hanoi

MA XO CAFE

Pull up a seat at this quaint 3-story café overlooking the lake. Each floor is staffed by an attentive and trendy young Vietnamese girl who is excited to interact with the foreign girl. I prefer the very top floor balcony for sipping a tea and pondering life, or the second-floor room with a big table great for working. Afterwards, take a walk along the lake and keep an eye out for fishermen pulling in the day's catch. Ps. Cash only!

☉ **Open:** Daily 8am-11:00pm
♥ **Where:** Truc Bac Lake
🚇 **Address:** 152 P. Trấn Vũ
♥ @ma.xo.cafe

LUNCH & DINNER

HONG HOAI RESTAURANT

Hungry foodies flock to Hong Hoai Restaurant in Hanoi for one dish in particular: Bun Cha. But this Bun Cha is special – it is made with a delicious western twist. Rather than ground pork patties, you are served glistening pieces of grilled pork on top of savory veggies with a side of lettuce, noodles, and Bun Cha broth. Hong Hoai calls themselves "Vietnamese Fusion" for putting a western spin on all their dishes…in other words, nothing weird. You can get your favorites like spring rolls, pho, and western dishes too. Clean eating with no surprises!

⊙ **Open:** Daily 10am-11pm
♥ **Where:** Old Quarter
🚅 **Address:** 20 Bát Đàn, Hàng Bồ, Hoàn Kiếm

BUN CHA HUONG LIEN AKA "OBAMA BUN CHA"

When former US President Barack Obama came to Hanoi, Anthony Bourdain took him to a local Bun Cha restaurant to enjoy some of the best Bun Cha in town. This was a HUGE deal and so…the restaurant is now referred to by locals as "Obama Bun Cha". This place is so extra that they memorialized the actual table and plates that the pair used by encasing them in glass and have hung framed photos of Obama all around. This spot is always bustling with locals and tourists often ordering "The Obama Combo". If this Bun Cha good enough for Obama, it's certainly good enough for you.

⊙ **Open:** 10am-7pm
♥ **Where:** North Hai Ba Trung
🚅 **Address:** 24 Le Van Huu

BÁNH MỲ 25

The 2nd best Banh Mi I've had in all of Vietnam (after Hoi An)! This small establishment has grown in popularity over the years for its generous fillings, creative combinations and…very easy to read English menu. Don't be fooled though. Just because the menu is in English doesn't make it any less authentic. You'll see both foreigners and locals flocking here as their quality is high, and prices are low! Get the roasted chicken Banh Mi with generous portions of chicken, veggies and a mayo sauce that is to die for. Order a beer or a milk tea to complete the experience.

⊙ **Open:** Daily 7am-9pm
📍 **Where:** Old Quarter
🏠 **Address:** 25 P. Hàng Cá, Hàng Bồ

BUN CHA 33 CO

When I lived in Hanoi, writing this book for the very first time, this was my go to "treat yourself" meal. Not because it's expensive (it's very cheap) but because eating here is an event! Noodles, meat, broth and fresh herbs just for you! This is by far the best bun cha I've had in Vietnam, and I've had a lot.

Sit down, hold up how many fingers of orders you want. They will ask you if you want spring rolls to dip. The answer is yes. Watch the people around you figure out how to eat bun cha but basically take a little noodles, a little meat and a little herbs and dip them in the broth with your chopsticks, and make it all into one bite. Note: Do not come here with more than 4 people, this place is tiny with plastic tables on the side of the street.

Ps. After lunch, walk around the back alleys. This is a neighborhood where not many foreigners go but where you are very safe. Before lunch, visit Doa Care massage, right down the street (you'll read about them soon)

⊙ **Open:** 7am-2pm
📍 **Where:** Hoang Hoa Neighborhood
🏠 **Address:** 269 d hoang hoa tham

BUN BO NAM BO

Alert: My favorite comfort food in Hanoi is this vermicelli bowl! There's something special about a restaurant that specializes in one dish...and they make it to utter perfection. A beefy broth with crunchy veggies, tender meat and gorgeous noodles- you won't know whether to call this a soup or a salad. Bún bò nam bộ is both and neither at the same time. It arrives on your table as a gorgeous, artistically displayed bowl of beauty- and then it's your job to mix it up into a smorgasbord of yum.

⊙ **Open:** Daily lunch to late
📍 **Where:** North West Old Quarter
🏠 **Address:** 1 P. Nguyễn Văn Tố

PHO GA SO 7

I love how tidy this place is! You can watch the chefs make your pho in a clean kitchen so you know that you're getting yummy chicken pho with no mystery or suspicion! The broth is so simple that the key is to make use of the garlic, lime, red chilis and liquid chili sauce to fancy it up. Get a big bowl of chicken pho for just around 45k!

⊙ **Open:** Daily 6:30am-2pm
📍 **Where:** Old Quarter
🏠 **Address:** Phở Gà Số 7 Hàng Buồm

....

MACHI RAMEN

A hipster ramen spot that is hidden in a maze of alleyways off the tourist path. These guys might be surprised to see you. The miso ramen is to die for. Although they don't sell alcohol, there is a local man next door who sells draft street beer next door for less than $1. Machi Ramen is cool with you ordering beer from this guy, making this the most unique ramen-in-Vietnam experience that you can get.

⊙ **Open:** Daily 10:30am-2pm / 5pm -9pm
📍 **Where:** Hoang Hoa Neighborhood
🏠 **Address:** số 26, Ng. 267 Đ

....

PHO GA SO 7

I love how tidy this place is! You can watch the chefs make your pho in a clean kitchen so you know that you're getting yummy chicken pho with no mystery or suspicion! The broth is so simple that the key is to make use of the garlic, lime, red chilis and liquid chili sauce to fancy it up. Get a big bowl of chicken pho for just around 45k!

⊙ **Open:** Daily 6:30am-2pm
📍 **Where:** Old Quarter
🏠 **Address:** Phở Gà Số 7 Hàng Buồm

....

PIZZA 4 P'S

I'm never going to stop talking about Pizza 4 P's. Ever. It's the most authentic pizza outside of Italy in... Vietnam of all places! There are 4Ps in Ho Chi Minh City, Da Nang, and Hanoi – all of which serve mind-blowing pizza with gobs of fresh mozzarella, hand tossed crust, and gourmet toppings. Some pizzas come served with a full fist-sized ball of fresh mozzarella which is unrolled to cover each slice of pizza at the table. For an extra special experience, call ahead to get a table at the wood fired oven where you can watch the pizzas being made to order.

Pro Tip: Make a reservation or just call ahead 1 hour to make sure they've got room!

⊙ **Open:** Daily 10am-10:30pm
📍 **Where:** District 1
🏠 **Address:** 8/15 Lê Thánh Tôn, Bến Nghé, Quận 1

STREET FOOD TOUR ON MOTORBIKE LED BY WOMEN

Jump on the back of a local girl's scooter as she zips you around Hanoi at night, taking you to try the best street food in the city. This takes the wondering ang guessing out of everything for you, as your guide explains exactly how each dish is made and why each particular stall is so special.

Book on Viator: Hanoi By Night Foodie Motorbike Tours

Ps. I love you and I'm proud of you! ♥

CHAPTER 1: HANOI

Nightlife in Hanoi

Night life seemingly never ends in Hanoi. You could be out all-night drinking, dancing, and bullshitting. Then order a Grab Taxi back home. It's a pretty safe city, so go for it.

OLD QUARTER - IN GENERAL

Old Quarter is filled with bars that go late into the night. Most people don't really go into it with a plan. They start with a bia hoi, mingle with others and then end up doing one of the following....

♥ Sip cocktails at Polite & Co.
♥ Drink til 4am at The Porch.
♥ Join the pub crawl at Vietnam Backpackers.
♥ Or just visit Beer Street and see what happens...

BEER STREET

Ta Hien Street is one narrow alley lined with Vietnamese restaurants selling food...and cheap beer. On warm weekend nights, this alley fills up with locals and expats alike. Mingling, eating, drinking, and buzzing with noise. Show up and see what calls you.

BIA HOI OR STREET BEER

You'll find Bia Hoi offered all over Vietnam; sometimes in a restaurant, sometimes at a hole in the wall…or best of all, just on the side of the road.

Most often, you can pull up a little plastic stool on the sidewalk, where you'll drink from the keg…. for around 25-50 cents per glass. Bia Hoi is the homemade brew that you'll find all over Vietnam- especially in Hanoi. Also called "fresh beer", there are no preservatives in this brew, so it must be consumed the same day that it's brewed.

While it only contains about 3% alcohol content – it goes down way too easy, so keep track of how many you knock back. Otherwise, the infamous 'Bia Hoi Hangover' awaits.

....

COOL SPOT ALERT!

The best place to drink Bia Hoi in Hanoi? Head to the Old Quarter and right across from Vietnam Backpacker Hostel, you'll find the cutest little lady with the biggest smile excited for you to pull up a seat. This is also a great place to meet other travelers as sometimes you're just thrown together by mama. She also has a chicken kebab sandwich that I didn't try but some British guys who have been coming here for 8 years all ordered one so they must be good.

⊙ **Open:** Late afternoon-mid morning
📍 **Where:** Old Quarter – Vietnam Backpacker Hostel Downtown
🏠 **Address:** 9 Mã Mây, Hàng Buồm, Hoàn Kiếm
📍 **Google Maps:**

....

BEST STREET BEER AND FOOD TOUR WITH LAN

There's a girl you just have to meet, her name is Lan. Lan is your immediate best friend who takes you to her favorite local hole-in-the-wall establishments that you'd never be able to approach on your own. These are places without menus you can't read! These are places where they've been brewing beer and cooking mama's secret recipes for decades. This is one of the coolest experiences in the city with one of my favorite people in the country.

Book here ☞

....

TRUNG HANG BEER RESTAURANT

This is where I used to take all my Bumble dates in Hanoi. It's a very local beer spot, so local that you'll see groups of businessmen in their suits getting wasted here at 4pm. It's great people watching but you need to know how the culture of this place works. Here's what happens: You sit down. You'll be asked if you want beer. You say yes. Then a little food elevator delivers you a pint of fresh beer from the second story. You'll be brought a bowl of peanuts. When you finish your beer, the waiter will gesture to you to see if you want more beer. The answer is yes. Beers will keep coming until you say no. You'll walk away shocked by how many beers you drank and how little money you spent. These beers are so cheap they're practically free.

PRO TIP: Trung Hang Beer Restaurant is close to Doa's Care Massage Spa and Bun Cha 3 Co. I recommend eating Bun Cha for lunch, walking to Doa's Care Massage Spa afterwards. Then walking to beer. It's a convenient little stroll between all three spots.

Open: Lunchtime - late
Where: Ba Dinh

Google Maps:

TRAVEL NOTES:

CHAPTER 1: HANOI

Sightseeing in Hanoi

Are you ready for all the temples, museums and monuments? Because Hanoi has all the temples, museums and monuments!

Heads up. There is a lot to see, so if you're a history buff that wants to absorb it all, take a tour.

HO CHI MINH MAUSOLEUM

This 21-meter high granite building houses the body of Vietnam's most iconic and influential leader, Ho Chi Minh, despite him specifically saying that he wanted to be cremated. Inspired by Lenin's own mausoleum, this building also contains elements of Vietnamese architecture. Tourists and locals alike go here to pay their respects to this leader. Be mindful of how you act as many Vietnamese consider this an important place to visit their beloved grandfather.

Because of its historical value, security is tight, and rules are strictly followed. A dress code is followed too, so don't go here wearing shorts, skirts, or tank tops. Lines usually stretch out pretty long, but don't get discouraged as it normally flows quickly and with no delay.

Budget: $1 USD / 20k VND
Open: Every day except Monday & Friday, 8:00am - 11:30am and 4:00pm - 16:30pm
Where: Ba Dinh Square

TEMPLE OF LITERATURE - VAN MIEU

A Temple of Confucius built almost a thousand years ago, the Temple of Literature is an astonishingly well-preserved piece of Vietnamese history. As the name might have given away, the Temple has been a place of learning for over 700 years. In fact, the Imperial Academy it houses was Vietnam's first national university. Today, it is one of Hanoi's most visited tourist attractions.

Explore the grounds that Confucius scholars and, on occasion, royalty, roamed centuries ago and experience the intricate Hanoi style architecture that Vietnam is known for. Divided into five courtyards, each section represents an era of Vietnamese architecture.

Budget: $1.3 USD / 30k VND
Open: Monday to Friday, 7.30am — 5.30pm; Weekend, 7:30am — 8.30pm
Where: P Quoc Tu Giam
Address: 58 Quoc Tu Giam, Van Mieu, Dong Da

BACH MA TEMPLE

A small building with yellow walls and a red gate, you could easily miss this beautiful temple, located in the heart of the old quarter. Built in the 11th century by Emperor Ly Thai To, Bach Ma or White Horse Temple, is the oldest temple in the city. Inside, there are glorious shrines and decorations, brightly-colored flags, and richly-painted columns. It's the perfect place for some peace and quiet with only the local's whispering their prayers and the smell of incense floating through the air.

💰 Budget: Free
🕒 Open:: Tuesday-Sunday 8.00am-11.00am; 2.00pm-5.00pm
📍 Where: Hanoi

PRO TIP! Ladies, cover your shoulders and knees when entering any temple or pagoda in order to show respect for Buddhist culture and the monks wandering the grounds.

VIETNAM MILITARY HISTORY MUSEUM

Notable as the Military Museum or Army Museum, Vietnam Military History Museum commemorates Vietnam's victories over the U.S. and French forces during the 20th century. The museum serves as one of the seven national museums in the country and one of the oldest museums located in Hanoi. Its wide collection of distinctive original artifacts makes it a cultural center for Vietnamese military history.

Spotting the museum is made easy with the display of a huge weaponry collection at the front. It also displays the U.S. and French weapons and the Chinese and Soviet equipment captured during warfare.

💰 Budget: $1.75 USD / 40k VND
🕒 Open: 8-11:30am & 1-4:30pm Tuesday-Thursday, Sat & Sunday
📍 Where: 28a P Dien Bien Phu
🏛 Address: Hanoi, Vietnam

HOA LO PRISON (THE HANOI HILTON)

The French built the Hao Lo prison in the late 19th century to house political prisoners and revolutionaries during the colonization of Vietnam. This prison is known as one of the most inhumane prisons in all of Asia, as you'll discover during your tour of tiny cells where Vietnamese were kept like animals, torture chambers, guillotines and more. You'll also see parts of the narrow pipe by which some prisoners were lucky enough to use as they fled from this hellhole.

But, instead of tearing down this monstrosity once the French abandoned post, the Vietnamese decided to continue the tradition of heinous torture within these walls- but on the Americans.

During the Vietnam War, Hoa Lo Prison became known as the "Hanoi Hilton" by American soldiers who were captured, held, and tortured by the communists. It's a gruesome yet poignant part of Vietnamese history, representing the battles, struggles, and revolutions that this country has endured and participated in.

The museum itself is not very big and you can tour the entire place within 30 minutes- which is probably all you can stomach anyways as some tourists report that they can actually feel heavy dread with every step.

Budget: $1.3 USD / 30k VND
Open: Daily 8:00am – 5:00pm (including festivals and holidays)
Where: Hoa Lo Street, French Quarter
Address: No. 1 Hoa Lo, Tran Hung Dao, Hoan Kiem District, Hanoi

QUÁN THÁNH TEMPLE

Classic. Historical. Unforgettable. Quán Thánh Temple is easily the most beautiful ancient architectural structure in all of Hanoi. With gray stone walls, adorned with intricate carvings, details, and elephant statues, utter silence seems appropriate as you absorb the peaceful history within these grounds. Enter through the majestic archway into an outdoor square lined with centuries old trees, leading to a traditional Buddhist shrine. Located right across the street, at the south end of the Tran Quoc Pagoda road, these two places (Tran Quoc Pagoda and Quán Thánh Temple) make for a great back-to-back sightseeing trip.

PRO TIP! Right outside of Quán Thánh Temple are a couple coffee shops selling coconut coffee and fresh coconuts which will round out your adventure perfectly.

💵 **Budget:** $.50 USD / 10k VND
🕒 **Open:** Daily 5am-7pm
📍 **Where:** Ba Dinh, across from the park at the south end of Thanh Nien Street

NGOC SON TEMPLE

Situated on a small islet in the middle of Hoan Kiem Lake of Hanoi, Ngoc Son Temple (also known as Temple of the Jade Mountain) is one of the prime tourist attractions. The temple was built in the 19th century and is dedicated to 13th Century Vietnamese military national hero General Tran Hung Dao. The temple is accessed via a quaint red wooden bridge named The Huc Bridge meaning the Bridge of the Rising Sun. This is a perfect place to start your day watching a spectacular sunrise in a quiet environment. The bridge leads to Dac Nguyet Lau meaning the "Moon Light tower" and Ngoc Son shrine.

The temple has 3 entrance gates in a series, depicting various Taoist symbols like tiger and Vietnamese dragon. There is a side room on the left of the main temple which has a preserved body of a giant soft backed turtle which was found in 1968. The temple grounds offer lovely views of the lake and the Turtle Pagoda. Together with Hoan Kiem Lake and the Tortoise Tower, Ngoc Son Temple is definitely a must visit place to enjoy Hanoi's age-old culture.

PRO TIP! The red bridge is accessible without needing to buy a ticket. The rest you'll need to pay the entrance fee.

💵 **Budget:** $1.3 USD / 30k VND
🕒 **Open:** Daily 8:00am – 6:00pm
📍 **Where:** Hoan Kiem Lake
🏛 **Address** Đinh Tiên Hoàng, Hàng Trống

TRAN QUOC PAGODA

The oldest pagoda in Hanoi, Tran Quoc Pagoda is over 1,405 years old. Built during the sixth century during the reign of Emperor Lý Nam Đế, this masterpiece is more than a piece of art; it is also the place of rest for many revered monks whose ashes lie inside. The pagoda is adorned with Buddhist symbolism with tranquil statues of buddha resting within the pagoda and lotus flower statues all around the property.

A true vision, this rusty red pagoda stands 15 meters tall or 11 stories high. Set between two large lakes, the pagoda reflects its image off the water, offering stunning mirror images that photographers will adore, especially in the mid-afternoon.

Budget: Free
Open: 7:30am-6pm
Where: Truc Bach area, on a tiny island floating on Westlake, connected by a walkable bridge.
Address Thanh Nien, Truc Bach, Ba Dình

GO TO A PARK IN THE MORNING

Hanoi at 6am is a totally different world. There are community Zumba classes, badminton games, old people doing Tai Chi, chess games, speed walkers, and of course…retired men sipping Vietnamese coffee while reading the newspaper. By 8am, everyone disappears like nothing ever happened.

Check out google maps, find the biggest park near you and you're bound to stumble upon fascinating old people activities. Some of my favorite parks to visit:

📍 Reunification Park
📍Lenin Park (Công viên Bách Thảo)

FUN FACT! You'll notice that buildings in Hanoi are tall but very narrow. That's because tax on property depends on how wide the building is! This gave these edifications the name of "tube houses".

 Hey, looking for recommendations and friends in Hanoi? Join this group for girls, Hanoi Beautiful

CHAPTER 1: HANOI

Markets & Shopping in Hanoi

ALL OF OLD QUARTER

Old Quarter is dense with stores selling knock off Under Armor and North Face gear alongside legit brand stores like Converse and Adidas. You'll find lots of souvenir knick knacks, shops selling bags of tea and coffee, and traditional Vietnamese dresses for humans of all ages. Just be ready to haggle. Any price you're given, counter with half the price. Never buy the first dress you like. Shop around and see what the average going rate is so that you get a good idea where your price point should be.

DONG XUAN MARKET

Hanoi's biggest indoor market offers 4-stories of everything from dried fruit to traditional Vietnamese dresses. As you wander around you'll notice that each section has its specialty: fabrics, baby clothes, shoes, and more. This market caters to both Vietnamese and Tourists – so even if you're not in the market for a wooden set of chopsticks, it's still fun to come and watch the madness. Located in Old Quarter, you can mosey on over here for a leisurely gander.

Open: Daily 7am-6pm
Where: Old Quarter

GoogleMaps:

QUANG BA FLOWER MARKET

While you may not have a practical use for fresh flowers while you're traveling through Hanoi, that doesn't mean that you don't have time to stop and smell the roses! Especially if you're an early riser. This place opens at 2am, featuring flowers from all across the country. Bring your camera!

⊙ **Open:** 24 hours - best time to visit is 9pm to midnight
Where: Tay Ho
Address: Au Co Street

GoogleMaps:

HANOI WEEKEND NIGHT MARKET

In terms of trinkets and souvenirs, the Hanoi Weekend Market is pretty standard. The cool part, however, is that the entire street is closed off to traffic, so you can wander and shop as you please. The ambiance is relaxing with glowing lights, while exhilarating with crowds of people as far as you can see. You'll definitely have one of those mental photo moments that you'll never forget. Plus, more street food vendors pop up, allowing for an unofficial food tour. If you're in the area, why not?

⊙ **Open:** Friday-Sunday 6pm- Midnight
Where: Old Quarter – Starts Hang Dao Street towards Dong Xuan Market

GoogleMaps:

CHO HOM MARKET

This 3-story market is a colorful playground for photographers and a fresh foodie's dream! The entire ground floor is packed with exotic fruit that you can buy and eat on the spot. Head upstairs to fabric heaven where several tailors have set up shop, ready to make you a classic Vietnamese dress or modern jacket. Just remember to haggle!

⊙ **Open:** Daily 6am-5pm
Where: Hai Ba Trung
Address: 293 Tran Nhan Tong, Hai Ba Trung District

GoogleMaps:

ROYAL CITY MALL

If you've worn your clothes down to holey rags, head on over to Royal City Mall where you can pop into stores like H&M, Levi's, Mangos, and Nike to freshen up that wardrobe. You'll find some coveted Korean Beauty stores here too like Skin Food and The Face Shop. This mall also has a decent food court and a gym if you want to make a day of it.

⊙ **Open:** Daily 10am-10pm
📍 **Where:** Royal City (20-30 minutes SouthWest of Old Quarter)
🏠 **Address:** Ngách 190/7, Thượng Đình, Thanh Xuân

📍 **GoogleMaps:**

WHAT ARE THESE?

The mesmerizing image of these colorful bundles has become such an iconic Vietnam postcard. At first glance, they look like flowers, but these are hundreds of incense sticks masterfully balanced to stand in these beautiful bouquets to dry in the sun. And all these bundles together, the are such a treat to the eye!

Incense making is a traditional common trade from Quang Phu Cau village, in the outskirts of Hanoi. This village produces around 50 tonnes of incense every month!

Check out this tour to see it for yourself ☞

CHAPTER 1: HANOI

Beauty & Wellness Guide to Hanoi

HAIR

SALON BLONDE

Blondes, Mitch is your man. This American artist turned Hanoi expat is king when it comes to blonde hair. He does gorgeous highlights, seamless touch ups…and most importantly, he is the man that girls run to when someone else has dyed their hair orange or cat piss yellow. He's got the magic touch, and in Asia- that is worth every god damn penny. Plus, his salon is just a lot of fun. Order delivery while you process, have a beer, join in on the gossip, and get some restaurant recommendations. And even if you're not in the market for color, treat yourself to a shampoo scalp massage and blow out.

Where: Truc Bach (gorgeous area for a stroll along the water)
Address: 104 A2 Luc Chính Truc Bach
facebook.com/SalonBlondeHanoi/

WAXING

HUE BEAUTY HOUSE CALLS

The most popular way to get waxed in Hanoi? Have your wax girl make a house call. Hue Pham is Hanoi's waxing extraordinaire! She comes to your hotel or house with all of her super clean waxing equipment in toe. She's got fresh Australian hot wax and accessories to wax any and everything. She'll lay a mat on the floor and clean you up for half the price of a salon. This was the most pain free Brazilian I've ever had. Also, important to note, when you get waxed at a salon, the girls who do the waxing only get 5-10% of the service price. The boss takes the rest. Home waxers in Hanoi are entrepreneurs who love what they do, take pride in what they do and can actually make a living wage.

Where: House/Hotel Calls
WhatsApp her here: +84 168 275 7993

🦷 TEETH | 🧴 SPAS

AUSTRALIAN DENTAL CLINIC

Okay, it's not a spa- BUT you can get your teeth cleaned by professionals for $12. They also do teeth whitening, cavity care, and even more intense procedures like full porcelain crowns and root canals. This is the place that expats from all around the world trust with their teeth and their wallet. Take advantage!

🕒 **Open:** Wednesday-Saturday 8:30am-7pm/Sunday 8:30am-5pm
📍 **Where:** Hai Ba Trung
🏠 **Address:** No 3 Nguyễn Du, Bùi Thị Xuân

f www.facebook.com/AustralianDentalClinic/

3 OTHER SPAS I RECOMMEND...

♥ **Doa Care** / daoscare.com
♥ **Hanoi Serene Spa** / serenespa.vn
♥ **La Belle Vie Spa** / hanoilabelleviespa.vn

PRO TIP FOR SPAS IN VIETNAM!

Know this - the cheaper the spa, the more they'll haggle you for a tip at the end.

OMAMORI SPA – VISUALLY IMPAIRED

An amazing spa with an amazing cause. All of the massage therapists at Omamori Spa are visually impaired. I say 'massage therapists' with emphasis, because these girls are professionally trained - a qualification that 90% of massage shops in Vietnam do not require. Omamori is run by a reputable non-profit whose goal is to empower those with disabilities.

Also, amazing: the 'no tipping policy' means no haggling and no shakedowns. These girls are compensated by commission AND profits by this amazing non-profit organization that is empowering the disabled while providing the most reputable and trustworthy spa services out there.

💰 **Starting at:** 300k for a 60-minute massage (plus no tip, this ends up being one of the cheapest places for a massage in Hanoi).
🕒 **Open:** Daily 9am-10pm
📍 **Where:** Old quarter
🏠 **Address::** 52A Hàng Bún, Quán Thánh, Ba Đình

CHAPTER 1: HANOI

From the Airport to Hanoi

Hanoi has an international airport that you can fly into from just about any location in Vietnam and outside of Vietnam.

Easy.

The journey to the city center usually takes around 30-45 minutes, depending on traffic conditions. Remember to have the name and address of your destination written down in Vietnamese or show it on a map to the taxi driver for easier communication.

Let us, however, discuss what to do once you land...✈✈✈

Quick video tutorial:

OPTION 1: GRAB TAXI

Once you're outside the airport, order a grab. They'll take you anywhere you need to go and help you with your bags.

Budget: Around $9 USD / 200k VND
Duration: 30-40 minutes

OPTION 2: THE BUS

Outside of Terminal 2 (T2), you can hop on a very cheap bus to the Old Quarter. Look for bus #17.

You board, tell the driver "Old Quarter" like 3x, and he'll tell you when to get off. Your stop is one of the last stops, called "Long Bien".

Once you're off the bus, it's a 5 to 10-minute walk to the Old Quarter. This is where having a SIM card comes in handy. Either order a Grab Taxi/Bike from the bus station to your hotel or walk it.

💸 **Budget:** $1.5 USD / 30k VND
🕑 **Open:** 60-90 minutes depending on traffic
📍 **Where:** Right outside of Terminal 2
🕑 **Times:** 6:18 am - 10:58 pm, every 20/30 minutes.

Ps. Here are all the Hanoi airport bus routes ☞

OPTION 3: AIRPORT TAXI

Taking a taxi is a popular and straightforward option. As you exit the airport terminal, you'll find official taxi counters where you can book a taxi at a fixed rate. The taxi companies you want to use are Mai Linh or Vinasun - to ensure a reliable and safe ride.

OPTION 4: AIRPORT SHUTTLE BUS

This option is suitable for budget-conscious travelers who don't mind a slightly longer travel time. Look for the signs or information desks at the airport to find the designated bus stops. The journey time can vary depending on the traffic, but it generally takes around 45 minutes to an hour to reach the city center.

CHAPTER TWO

Ha Giang

BEST FOR:

3 days/4 nights

DAYS NEEDED:

Riding on the back of a locals motorbike as you have one of the top 5 most unforgettable experience of your life, driving through awe-inspiring hills, staying at fascinating homestays, seeing life off the beaten path, and connecting with a region of Vietnam only recently accessible to the outside word.

HA GIANG

CHAPTER TWO

Ha Giang

One of the most remote regions on Earth near the border of China, Ha Giang is a region where time seemingly stands still. Isolated villages that are a 3-day drive into the mountains, mind-blowing valleys where few humans have ever stood, and human connections so pure that your heart will grow 3 sizes. Ha Giang is a once in a lifetime trip. And to access it, you need two wheels.

The "Ha Giang Loop" is typically a 3-5-day motorbiking adventure through windy mountain hills where each day your only goal is to make it to the next village for a warm bed, home cooked meals, and rice wine shared with new friends. As you wind your way through the loop to your next destination, you'll be treated to awe-inspiring panoramas at every turn while saying "wow" under your breath all day long.

If I could stress one place that you should absolutely visit in all of Vietnam, this would be it.

PRO TIP! Don't ride on your own. My big bad boyfriend wanted to ride his own motorbike, and was disappointed when the company we chose insisted that he had a motorbike license to drive. So my big 6'2 boyfriend got on the back of a Vietnamese guy's bike for the journey. A couple hours into the winding terrain, my boyfriend was very happy to be a passenger and not a driver.

While riding the Ha Giang Loop on the back of a local's motorbike may sound thrilling, it's important to prioritize safety. Make sure to choose a reliable and experienced driver who knows the region well. They can guide you through the winding roads and ensure you have a safe and enjoyable journey. So let's talk about the two best companies to travel with:

HA GIANG ADVENTURES

This is who I chose for my once-in-a-lifetime experience. Owned by Cuong, a Hanoi boy and social entrepreneur whose goal is to benefit the communities he sends you to. Rather than just "tourism", he is offering you a local experience that feels good and is in harmony with the culture.

Yes, this trip is a little pricier than the next - but it's private, it's safe, and it's an experience you'll be talking about forever (seriously, I tell everyone I meet who is going to Vietnam to do this).

♥ Pick Up: In Hanoi around 6am, where you'll be taken straight to Ha Giang to have lunch and get on the back of a bike.

JASMINE HOSTEL

The cheaper option and the more social option. We passed groups of up to 25 motorbikes driving together like a mountain gang, Vietnamese driving and foreigners on the back. The groups would stop at coffee shops and hang out with each other then carry on to the next spot. The upside is that this trip is affordable and you will make friends. The downside is that you'll move a little more slowly depending on the group size, and this trip does get tiring.

To Get to Ha Giang, you'll start in Hai Phong and take an 11-hour night bus then head over to Jasmine Hostel.

♥ **Book here:** https://jasminehagiang.com/

BEST AND WORST TIME OF YEAR FOR THE TRIP

→ **Worst Time:** May to September (Rainy season) - Heavy rains, slippery roads, landslides, and reduced visibility make the trip challenging and hazardous. You do not want to do this trip when it's raining. You will be miserable.

→ **Good Time:** October to April (Dry season) - Pleasant weather, clear skies, lush landscapes, perfect for motorbike travel.

→ **Best Time:** The most beautiful time to visit Ha Giang, with emerald green rice fields and less rain, is in September and October. The weather is generally dry and stable during this period, allowing for a safer and more enjoyable motorbike trip.

NOTES ON WEATHER:

I went in February and was a bit cold, so pay attention to my packing list next.

CHAPTER 2: HA GIANG

What to Pack for Ha Giang

Everything I discuss will be in my Ha Giang Packing List

☞ Alexa-West.com/OneWay

High elevation means cold temperatures. Your company should provide you with gloves. Besides that, here's what to bring.

✓ A small backpack or duffle: Whatever you bring will be strapped onto the back of your motorbike. I took only the zip-off backpack from my Osprey 55 liter backpack.

✓ Layers: Long johns top and bottom, down zip-up jacket and a water resistant windbreaker shell. If you're going in rainy season, waterproof pants.

✓ For the Ride: Yoga Pants or sweatpants.

✓ For Sleep: Yoga pants or sweatpants + a sweatshirt + a t-shirt.

✓ Shoes: Closed toed sneakers and a pair of Teva-like water shoes.

✓ Sunglasses and a swimsuit

✓ Compression Bag: To compress these bulky items so they fit in your bag.

✓ A Mini-Speaker: You need music on the back of the bike! Get the speaker in my blog and save my Ha Giang Playlist!

✓ Snacks like granola bars or crackers. Best that you bring these from home.

HA GIANG OR SAPA?
People often ask me which is better. Answer: **Ha Giang, if being on a motorbike sounds fun**, is a once-in-a-lifetime experience but a rugged experience. **If you want more comfort, trekking or even luxury, Sapa.**

CHAPTER THREE

Sapa

DAYS NEEDED:

3-5 days

BEST FOR:

Mountain trekking and indigenous culture

CHAPTER THREE

Sapa

For years, this region represented the mystical fairy tales that we only believed to exist in fairytales (or before the invention of plastic).

With winding mountain roads, lush tropical rainforests, rolling hills for miles, and not a skyscraper in sight, Sapa is the epitome of pure nature. The land before time.

Only until the past 20 years or so, Sapa has been a town isolated from the rest of the world. Located in the Hoang Lien Son mountain range near the Chinese border, this northwestern Vietnamese region is full of locals living off the land and children who make a living by hauling rocks up the mountain roads instead of going to school.

Representing ethnic minorities, life in Sapa has always been more primitive than the rest of Vietnam. Homestays, treks, cooking over fire- this is what attracted westerners from near and far to come and marvel at a world once forgotten. And marvel they did.

The bittersweet result is that this sudden influx of tourism has transformed Sapa. Before tourism, the locals desperately struggled with poverty. And now...they still struggle with poverty but have come to rely on money from tourism.

You'll be introduced to five of Vietnam's ethnic minority tribes here: Black Hmong, Red Dzao, Tay, Giáy, Thai, and Phù Lá.

These locals have started setting up more homestays, more treks, and are selling more weed. For a while, this was manageable with a happy medium. But you'll notice that in the center of town, the locals are literally money hungry.

The Sapa tourist scene can be a bit overwhelming, at first. To reach the unspoiled nature treks and to get totally off the grid, you first must battle hawkers tugging on your clothes trying to sell you a tour or guest houses giving you misleading information that sways you to sign up with their bus company.

The innocence is gone. But the beauty remains. That is why this chapter is particularly important as it's filled with trust-worthy guest houses, money-saving tours, and 'what to expect' advice. Because once you make it past the 'wall of sales', there's no denying how magical Sapa really can be.

Also, make sure you pack for the weather as thick fogs are known to block tourists in their trails. Their billboard "Four seasons in one day" is no joke as it can literally go from freezing winters to tropical summers within the day. Do a bit of research before you come so that you can dress accordingly.

CHAPTER 3: SAPA

Areas to Know in Sapa

THE MAIN VILLAGE OF SAPA

The base camp for all of your adventures! If you've ever been to Pai, Thailand- that's kind of what to expect in the Main Village of Sapa. The main road is called Pho Cau May, where you'll find plenty of guest houses, and a couple upscale hostels surrounded by little restaurants and brightly colored souvenir shops. All of this dropped right in the middle rolling green mountains and lush rainforest. There's even a big lake where you can take a little boat out for a little paddle.

There are tour offices, places to drink, and locals always selling a service or a trinket. While the main village is a sight in itself.... this is just the beginning.

THE MAIN TREKKING DESTINATIONS

Sapa is the adventure capital of the north and offers lots of interesting trekking options, giving you an insight into local villages, valleys and rice fields. Grab a guide and head for the hills, it's time to explore Sapa's remotest regions.

CAT CAT VILLAGE

Home to the Black Hmong, Cat Cat Village is a beautiful village located about 3 km from Sapa and presents an easy and rewarding trek to visit a village famed for its traditional handicrafts. The Black Hmong are weavers and you will be able to see numerous craftspeople at work throughout the village. You can also purchase these goods at the numerous stores dotted around the village.

TA PHIN VILLAGE

Located 17 km from Sapa, Ta Phin is the village of the Red Dao people and has remained unchanged for centuries. The Red Dao are famed for their textile work and the village is known to supply most of the shops in Hanoi and Ho Chi Minh with brocade work dresses and silks. The workers do not stop and will negotiate prices and sales with you whilst still weaving, a tradition that goes back centuries to ensure they remain productive at all times. Ta Phin is a challenging trek from Sapa due to the condition of the roads but can be easily accomplished by motorbike.

LAO CHAI VILLAGE

Lao Chao is another village made up almost exclusively of Black Hmong people and serves as a great resting spot for those on the longer trek to Tavan. The village has become famous as a great place to get a little downtime on the challenging trek to Tavan and offers some great local foods and the opportunity to purchase the weaved handicrafts the Black Hmong are famous for. Lao Chai Village is roughly 7 km from Sapa.

BAN HO VILLAGE

Ban Ho is home to the Tay people and is known for its scenic beauty and slightly warmer climate than Sapa. The Muong Hoa river runs through the valley that the Tay people call home and helps them irrigate their farmland. The Tay are known to be great farmers and grow crops of rice and beans that they trade with the other local tribes. The beautiful scenic route to Ban Ho valley is roughly 25 km from Sapa, but makes for a rewarding trek due to the nature of the lush valley that Ban Ho Village sits in.

TA VAN VILLAGE

Ta Van is located at the bottom of the valley just along from Lao Chai and is known for being best accessed by jeep due to the nature of the narrow, dirt roads leading to the bottom of the valley. Tavan is home to the Giay people who are the area's main rice farmers and supply a number of the region's towns and cities. The Giay are also famed for their silver crafts and for the quaint stilt houses that are dotted around their village.

HEAVEN'S GATE

Take a breathtaking drive along the mountain road called Tram Ton Pass, which is the highest mountain pass in all of Vietnam at 1900 meters. On your journey, you'll zoom by bright green rice fields, vast valleys, and rolling hills along the way until you get to what the locals call "Heaven's Gate"- a gorgeous rock face with a unique window that when light shines through, looks like a portal to another world. You'll either need to rent a motorbike to her here or hire a guide and hop on the back of his bike.

CHAPTER 3: SAPA

Where to Stay in Sapa

The whole allure of Sapa is to have a local experience in a local homestay. Go on a trekking tour and you'll be led to a local's homestay where you'll eat home cooked meals and get a glimpse into local life. I've also thrown in a couple luxury retreats to soothe those legs of yours after all that trekking...

TOPAS ECOLODGE

Excuse my language, but holy f*cking shit. GET IT, GIRL. This frankly stunning hotel nestled in the mountains rocks your world with clean, design focused rooms, friendly staff and quite possibly one of the most gorgeous infinity pools you will ever come across. Just go here, love it and then tell everyone you know that you went there; making people jealous isn't just confined to social media, right?

Budget: $$$$
Where: Outside Sapa –
The Ecolodge will arrange transport

Book Here:

INDI HOUSE

A stay at Indi House feels akin to a detox retreat for the mind, body, and soul. Rustic wooden cabins surrounded by green rolling hills and fresh air is just what you need to press the restart button on life! This local run homestay offers functional rooms with great terraces or balconies, plus beautiful gardens to wander in after a hard day trekking.

Budget: $$
Where: Ta Van

Book Here:

LAXSIK ECOLODGE

This enchanting eco-friendly retreat offers a perfect blend of nature and cultural immersion. Wake up to stunning mountain views from your cozy bungalow and start the day with farm-fresh breakfasts sourced from the lodge's organic gardens. Laxsik Ecolodge's commitment to sustainability shines through community-driven initiatives, ensuring your visit positively impacts the environment and local community.

Go trekking with the H'mong people then come back to relax in the pool and end your evening with fellow travelers by the bonfire under the stars. Laxsik Ecolodge books up often so book it soon!

Budget: $$$
Where: 15-minute drive from Sapa Town   **Book Here:**

BAC HA THREELAND HOMESTAY

Want to visit the Bac Ha market? Stay here. Mr Son and his wife, Mrs Nagn, are the best homestay hosts on the planet who will make you feel like you're their long lost child coming home from college to visit. They'll make you food, help you arrange your adventures and transportation and are the support system to lean on if you're having travel troubles. Their beautiful home overlooks the green farmlands, tucked away from the hustle and bustle of Sapa town, but still a 20-minute stroll into town. You won't regret staying here. These are your parents on the other side of the world who will help you make the most out of your Sapa experience.

PRO TIP! Ask them about their trekking tours where you'll spend one night or more in the hills of Sapa. Book with them first, then use Booking.com's chat feature to get more info.

Budget: $$
Where: Near Bac Ha Market, not Sapa   **Book Here:**

PAVI HOME

If you're traveling with a friend and on a budget, book this place! You can split the price of the double room and have a sleepover. Go hiking the next morning, cuddle with their pets on site and enjoy all the outdoor seating that gives you the opportunity to journal, ponder and unwind surrounded by nature. This place is clean and crisp and dare I say, a little trendy - so if you're looking for a homestay with a glam touch, this is the place for you.

Budget: $$
Where: Ta Van

Book Here:

SAPA MOUNTAIN QUEEN HOUSE

Want to stay smack-dab in the center of Sapa town amongst the sights and near transportation? This is it. You're just a 5-minute walk to the center of town where you can shop, eat and explore the lake. Your host, Mr. Kim loves to cater to his guests every need! This is a 4-star hotel but has the hospitality of a Sapa homestay. This is a great option if you're transitioning to or from another homestay in the mountains.

Budget: $$
Where: Sapa Town

Book Here:

SURELEE HOMESTAY

The homestay for solo travelers that want to meet people and make friends. Family-style dinners mean instant connection over home cooked meals in the evening, and staying up with a beer chatting about your adventures. Another bonus is the price! Surelee Homestay is one of the best values you will find. The price is cheap but you get million-dollar views! That's because this homestay is located on a steep hill outside of town, so get ready to hike! The extra benefit here though is that once you arrive, you can explore by yourself and/or join a trekking tour with your hosts and other guests.

Budget: $
Where: Ta Van

Book Here:

MEKHOO & ZIZI SAPA HOMESTAY

Located on the mountainside 8km from Sapa this cute and spotlessly clean homestay drops you right into the mix with the local hill-tribes and is superbly located for trekking around Sapa's valleys. They also offer you the opportunity to participate in volunteer classes to improve the education of the local people and can put you in touch with local guides and can organize some longer-term treks into the forests. They also whip up incredible family style meals at the end of the day while you rest up those weary "trekked out" legs!

Budget: $
Where: Hau Thao

Book Here:

FUN FACT! The name Vietnam comes from two words: Viet and Nam. "Viet" was used in ancient Chinese to describe a foreigner, and "Nam" meant toward the South. So it's believed that the name Vietnam was born as a refernece of "people from the South".

CHAPTER 3: SAPA

Where to Eat in Sapa

When you're in the hills, you'll eat at your homestay. But when you're in town, you'll find tons of restaurants lining Pho Cau May, the main road in Sapa's central village. There are plenty of places for coffee, Vietnamese food, local dishes, and pizza! Prices are reasonable and portions generally huge, so roll up your sleeves and dive in! Here are a couple favorites in town...

GOOD MORNING VIETNAM RESTAURANT

Huge portions and lots of laughs at this family run favorite. Good Morning Vietnam is an ever present when it comes to Sapa's "top eats" list and it's easy to see why at this place. The service is incredible; with friendly staff happy to make suggestions and great value to be had all round. The menu is extensive and takes in traditional Vietnamese favorites and more local Hmong specialties. The Coconut Curry is their specialty and order after order seems to stream from the kitchen doors.

◎ **Open:** 8:30am-10:30pm
📍 **Where:** Sapa Town
🏠 **Address:** 063 B Fanxipan

MOMENT ROMANTIC RESTAURANT

The views of the Hoang Lien Mountain are breathtaking and complement this restaurant's slightly more upmarket vibe. The restaurant is small, but really well laid out and the staff (who speak excellent English) really seem to care about your meal. It's a little pricey than elsewhere but when those plates drop you'll understand why. The care and attention to detail at Moment Romantic is spot on. Always full and always tasty; fuel up here and you won't be disappointed. Their fried spring rolls are beyond incredible.

◎ **Open:** 8am-10pm
📍 **Where:** Sapa Town
🏠 **Address:** 026 Muong Hoa Street, TT. Sa P

CHAPTER 3: SAPA

Nightlife in Sapa

With most visitors hunkered down in homestays and getting drunk on rice wine with the locals – there isn't a huge nightlife scene here...except for these rare gems...

THE H'MONG SISTERS

This relaxed and fun pub serves up great cocktails and ice-cold beer. The atmosphere is a lot more relaxed than some of the other bars on this list and is a good place to unwind after a hard day on the trails. Locals like to come here and swap stories about their monster hikes too, so it's fun to grab a seat and listen in. They also have a pool table and a great buy-one-get-one free happy hour (4pm-7pm) every day.

Open: 4pm-1am
Where: Sapa Town
Address: 31 Muong Hoa

MOUNTAIN BAR AND PUB

This place serves up incredibly strong cocktails, super cheap beers and really gets the place rocking with table football tournaments most nights. Mountain Bar seems to always be buzzing with something going on and tends to score pretty highly on Sapa's "go to nightlife" list. Grab a seat and join the fun!

Open: 2pm-11:30 (open till 2am on Saturday and Sunday)
Where: Sapa
Address: 02 Muong Hoa Road

CHAPTER 3: SAPA

Best Things to Do in Sapa

VISIT BAC HA MARKET

Big Tip for Sapa: Schedule your trip to overlap on a Sunday so that you can visit the famous Bac Ha Market where ethnic communities living in Lao Cai Province (80 km from Sapa Town) gather to exchange and trade goods only on Sundays. Expect livestock everywhere, people in traditional dress and food to eat. Be prepared for lots of color, noise and animals, dead and alive! It's easy to spend three hours or more just wandering, eating and taking pictures. You've never seen anything like this.

⚑How to get there: Bac Ha is not in Sapa. It's a 2-3 hour bus ride away, however, there are shuttle buses between Lao Cai (the terminal where all travelers arrive via train to go to Sapa) and Bac Ha, and shuttle buses between Sapa and Bac Ha. So here's how we bundle Bac Ha with Sapa.

<u>Hanoi - Bac Ha - Sapa Itineraries:</u>

→ Take the overnight train on Thursday or Friday from Hanoi to Lao Cai.
→ Upon arrival, take a shuttle bus to Bac Ha and stay overnight at Bac Ha Homestay.
→ Spend your free days trekking, exploring and relaxing.
→ Wake up early Sunday morning and make your way to the market.
→ Take a shuttle from Bac Ha to Sapa.
→ Spend Sunday night in Sapa.
→ Trek on Monday and Tuesday
→ Then take a shuttle that evening back to Lao Cai and take the overnight train to Hanoi.

Or you can...

→ Take the train Friday night.

→ Arrive in Lao Cai on Saturday morning.

→ Stay in Lao Cai Saturday.

→ Sunday morning take a shuttle bus from Lao Cai to Bac Ha.

→ Explore the market then jump on a shuttle bus (located in Bac Ha) to Sapa.

→ Spend a day or a few days in Sapa, trekking and relaxing.

→ When you're ready to leave, take an evening shuttle back to Lao Cai and take the overnight train to Hanoi.

More about the Bac Ha Shuttle Buses:

From Lao Cai Terminal

Times: 6:30 a.m., 7am, 11 a.m., and 1 p.m (don't be surprised if these buses are late)
How Much: 60,000 VND
Duration: About 2 hours

From Sapa

Times: Wait for a mini bus in front of the church
How Much: 50,000 VND
Duration: 2-3 hours

PRO TIP! Visit Mr Nghe at Green Sapa tour who will help you arrange hotel pick-up from Sapa

Traveling by train and want to go directly to Bac Ha? Here is an alternative route? Skip Lao Cai. Get off at Pho Lu station, which is only 50 km away from the market. When you arrive, hire a local taxi or motorbike to take you. (Best to be traveling with a backpack for this one).

Confident on a motorbike? From Sapa, you can rent a motorbike for around 100 VND a day and crusie the dreamy hills on the way to Bac Ha for about 40-50 km, turning left at the three-way crossroad leading to Bac Ha.

TREKKING

The heavenly valleys, the unspoiled wildlife, the isolated villages, the clean air...trekking in Sapa is a humbling and life-changing experience. There are so many treks that you can sign up for; some of which last for 4 hours and some of which last for 4 days.

Here's the Trick to Trekking in Sapa:

Look through the trekking options at your hotel or a local tourist office. Take a picture of the page, if you'd like. And then.... go find a local to take you on that very same trek. Why? Here's a little scenario....

Let's say you get a local guide named Lek via your hotel. Your hotel hires Lek to take you on a 4-hour trek for the price of $60, BUT the hotel will most likely pay Lek just $15.

Alternatively, you can go find Lek on your own and haggle your price down to $45. Lek gets to keep every penny and is happy as a clam. You can even ask Lek to take you back to his family's home for lunch!

Just make sure you work out a round-trip deal, whether that is your guide trekking back with you or a taxi coming to pick you back up.

PRO TIP! Sapa is extremely safe in terms of crime. Trust is inherent and there are no reports of violence towards travelers. You're okay to hire a local to trek into the wilderness with. If you feel uncomfortable, ask around for some other travelers who are interested in a group trek.

BRING SCHOOL SUPPLIES TO VILLAGE SCHOOLS

The most rewarding day that you'll ever have in Vietnam is when you get to deliver pencils, notepads, erasers, or even toothbrushes to the isolated ethnic minority schools. Hire a motorbike driver to take you or seek out a trekking tour that will take you past a school that is a 3-day hike away from town. These schools need all the help they can get.

DO A HOME STAY

Homestay sleeps can actually be quite comfortable with big heavy blankets to keep you warm during the night and incredible views to wake up to. An overnight homestay usually includes all of your meals, a trekking guide, local village tours, and an all around memorable experience. To choose a homestay, either pick a trekking distance you can handle, a village that seems extra interesting, or a guide who you just have a good feeling about- and go. I've also listed a few popular homestays in our 'accommodation' section. If you come across the opportunity, the Red Dao Village is a cool experience as this community specializes in herbal medicine, with some homestays offering herbal baths and treatments.

PRO TIP! These homestays are run by ethnic minorities, whom the mainstream Vietnamese don't have much compassion for. Keep in mind, when you buy a homestay trek from a Vietnamese company (rather than a local minority), the Vietnamese company gives the bare minimum to the local guide who houses you, feeds you, and cares for you.

HMONG COOKING CLASSES

How does smoked buffalo sound to you? What about tofu from scratch? When you take a Hmong cooking class, you'll learn how to make a 5-course meal using fresh ingredients from the region. Sign up for the 7am cooking class, where you'll join your Hmong chef on an errand to the market. You'll collect all your ingredients and return to a beautifully clean kitchen to learn how to cook like a Hmong step-by-step. After you cook, sit down and enjoy your meal like a mountain queen, wine and all. You'll find these classes being offered by local Hmong people and guesthouses. Take your pick.

FANSIPAN MOUNTAIN

The highest peak in Indochina, Fansipan Mountain, is 3,143 meters of pure Earth just waiting for you to climb it...or cable car it.4

You can either trek up the mountain with a guided tour or take an exhilarating cable car ride up to the top. The cable car ride is a better idea if rigorous trails and hiking gear don't appeal to you.

No matter how you get there, once at the top, you'll be greeted with 'top of the world' views along with crisp air and an unforgettable sense of accomplishment.

For the cable car, you'll be riding with Sun World Fansipan Legend. Get a motor taxi to the cable car platform from town.

Budget: $30 USD /700k VND Round Trip
Where: Includes the "Funicular" train that takes you to the Fansipan Terminal so that you can avoid walking up 600 steps to the cable car platform.
Address: Nguyen Chi Thanh Street

SAPA CULTURE MUSEUM

Learn about the history and mythology of the local tribes at this free to enter cracker of a museum. The exhibits aim to help you understand the differences between the hill-tribes and showcase local handicrafts.

Budget: Free, but donations are appreciated (and needed)
Open: Daily, 7:30am-11:30am, 1:30pm-5pm
Address: TT. Sa Pa, Lao Cai

Ps. Have you signed up for my Travel Tips newsletter yet?

CHAPTER 3: SAPA

Markets & Shopping in Sapa

Buy local! If you see something you like in the shops, you can ask a local to take you to the source. Not only does this make a better story, but you are giving 100% of the profits to the local handicraftsman.

SAPA MARKET

Tribespeople from the local area converge on Sapa daily to sell their handicrafts and warm clothing. The prices are tourist focused, but haggling is expected. The food stalls are open for breakfast and lunch and offer hearty, filling trekker friendly local cuisine. Saturday tends to be the busiest day so get there early for the best bargains.

⊙ Open: 6am-6pm
Address: QL4D, TT. Sa Pa, Lao Cai

PRO TIP! Any fabric or trinket made with blue dye will stain your fingers and clothes. You'll actually see local women with blue fingers. Take note from them.

Want more markets?

Ask your hosts to help you organize a visit to one of these local markets…

→ Visit Coc Ly on Tuesday

→ Cao Son on Wednesday

→ Can Cau on Saturday

CHAPTER 3: SAPA

Crime & Safety in Sapa

Sapa is very safe. Attacks, assaults, and robberies are rare.

There are, however, a couple things to watch out for.

RENTING A MOTORBIKE FROM LOCALS

They will ask for your Passport or $250 deposit...which are usually fine in bigger cities but when you're renting from a local, you have no real terms of action if something goes wrong.

PETTY THEFT

Kids are sneaky. Keep your purse zipped while out and about. Bring a lock and key to keep your big backpack impenetrable when you leave it at a homestay while you play with chickens and cows.

RUGGED TERRAIN

Walking and riding a motorbike on rocky mountains and muddy hills presents the opportunity for slipping. Wear appropriate shoes and don't trek drunk!

Say it with me, now... "Travel Insurance".

Visit me here at Alexa-West.com/OneWay ♥

CHAPTER 3: SAPA

Insider Tips for Sapa

BRING CLOTHES MADE FOR MOUNTAIN WEATHER

The higher elevation offers colder temperatures, especially at night. Bring a poncho or a jacket. Don't have one? You can buy one in Sapa. If you plan to go trekking, bring hiking shoes or rubber boots. You can also rent these from trekking offices.

BUY FROM ADULTS, NOT KIDS

Kids are cute, and the local families have caught on that tourists agree! Because tourists have big hearts, they often can't say no when a child comes up to them selling trinkets. But you must say no. Do not encourage the practice of children begging. Do not incentivize these families to pull their children from school in order to make a living on the street.

DON'T SAY "MAYBE LATER"

This is as good as "Yes, please" when trying to get hawkers to leave you alone. On your treks, you'll be followed by kids trying to sell you things. They can be relentless little hustlers, so "maybe later" is just more incentive to keep trying.

DO NOT GIVE KIDS CANDY

You'll see signs around the town in English that encourage locals not to give the children sugary treats. The kids here have terrible dental health which is perpetuated by the casual import of sugar by good-intentioned tourists. Instead, bring stickers!

DO BUY FROM OLD LADIES

Like grandmas everywhere, you'll find old women from ethnic minority tribes who have kept the tradition of hand weaving alive. These women sell blankets, scarves, and bags made with their own two hands. You'll come across these women in town, in the villages, along local paths- it's all good.

BUY LOCAL

Buy trinkets from local hands instead of the shops. And go on treks by hiring your own guide on the street, rather than a trek from your hotel which typically gives the guides just 20% of the profits for their hard day's work.

ACCIDENTS HAPPEN

Muddy hills can lead to falls and scrapes and sprains. The hospitals around here are very basic. The hospitals around here can provide temporary care, but for bigger accidents, head to Lao Cai Hospital (38 kms away).

CHAPTER 3: SAPA

How to Get to Sapa

FROM HANOI

Hanoi is the most convenient jumping off point for Sapa, unless you're driving a motorbike.

By car: 4-5.5 hours on average from Hanoi to Sapa via highway CT05.

By bus: Approximately 5.5-6 hours for the trip from Hanoi to Sapa.

By train: 8 hours from Hanoi to Lao Cai (the nearest railway station to Sapa). From Lao Cai Train Station, an additional 65 minutes by road to reach Sapa town.

BY BUS

The bus is very windy as it goes up twisting mountain roads, but also very scenic. If you get motion sickness, ask to sit in the front seat and bring motion sickness pills. There is no toilet on the bus, but it will make stops along the way.

♀ Point of Departure:
⊙ When: Multiple times per day but it's best to take a morning bus around 7am.
⊙ Duration: 5.5-6 Hours
💵 Budget: $12-$17

PRO TIP! If you book with Sapa Express Bus, they will pick you up directly from your hotel or hostel in the Old Quarter of Hanoi.

BY SLEEPER TRAIN

You are traveling from Hanoi to Lao Cai Station.

The sleeper train is comfortable with sleeper beds, a dining car, and bathrooms. It will take you to Lao Cai Station, which is 35 kilometers from Sapa. Once you get into Lao Cai Station, there will be multiple shuttle buses waiting to take you into Sapa for less than 100k VND.

♀ Point of Departure: Hanoi Station to Lao Cai Station
⊙ When: There are multiple night trains that leave around 9:30-10pm
⊙ Duration: 8-9 hours
💵 Budget: $40-$80

PRO TIP! Buy your train ticket from the train station or 12Go.Asia a few days in advance so you can avoid paying marked up tourist office prices. Ask for a top bunk. As you'll be sharing a car with 3 other strangers, the top bunk will make you feel a bit safer as you slumber.

HELPFUL TIPS FOR TRAVELING TO SAPA:

→ **Book Your Train Tickets Wisely:** Ensure you book your train tickets from Hanoi Railway Station (not Yen Vien or Gia Lam) for a smoother journey.

→ **Opt for VIP or First-Class Tickets:** For added privacy, consider booking VIP class or first-class tickets, which are reasonably priced and offer fewer beds in each car, reducing the chance of sharing with strangers.

ARRIVING IN LAO CAI AND GETTING TO SAPA

BY BUS

After arriving in Lao Cai, hop on a bus to reach the captivating town of Sapa.

⊙**Departure Times:** Buses depart frequently, starting from 5.30 am and continuing every 20-30 minutes throughout the day until around 4 pm.

⊙**Duration:** The bus journey to Sapa typically takes around 1.5 hours.

Budget: Bus tickets cost 50,000 VND and can be purchased either onboard or in advance online via Baolau (recommended during peak seasons and holidays/weekends) for a hassle-free experience.

RETURNING TO HANOI FROM SAPA

Catch the red and yellow public bus (#2) from outside Sapa church to reach Lao Cai railway station.

Next, board the night train departing from Lao Cai at 10:30 pm and arriving in Hanoi at 5:25 am.

To secure your night train ticket in advance, you can book it here:

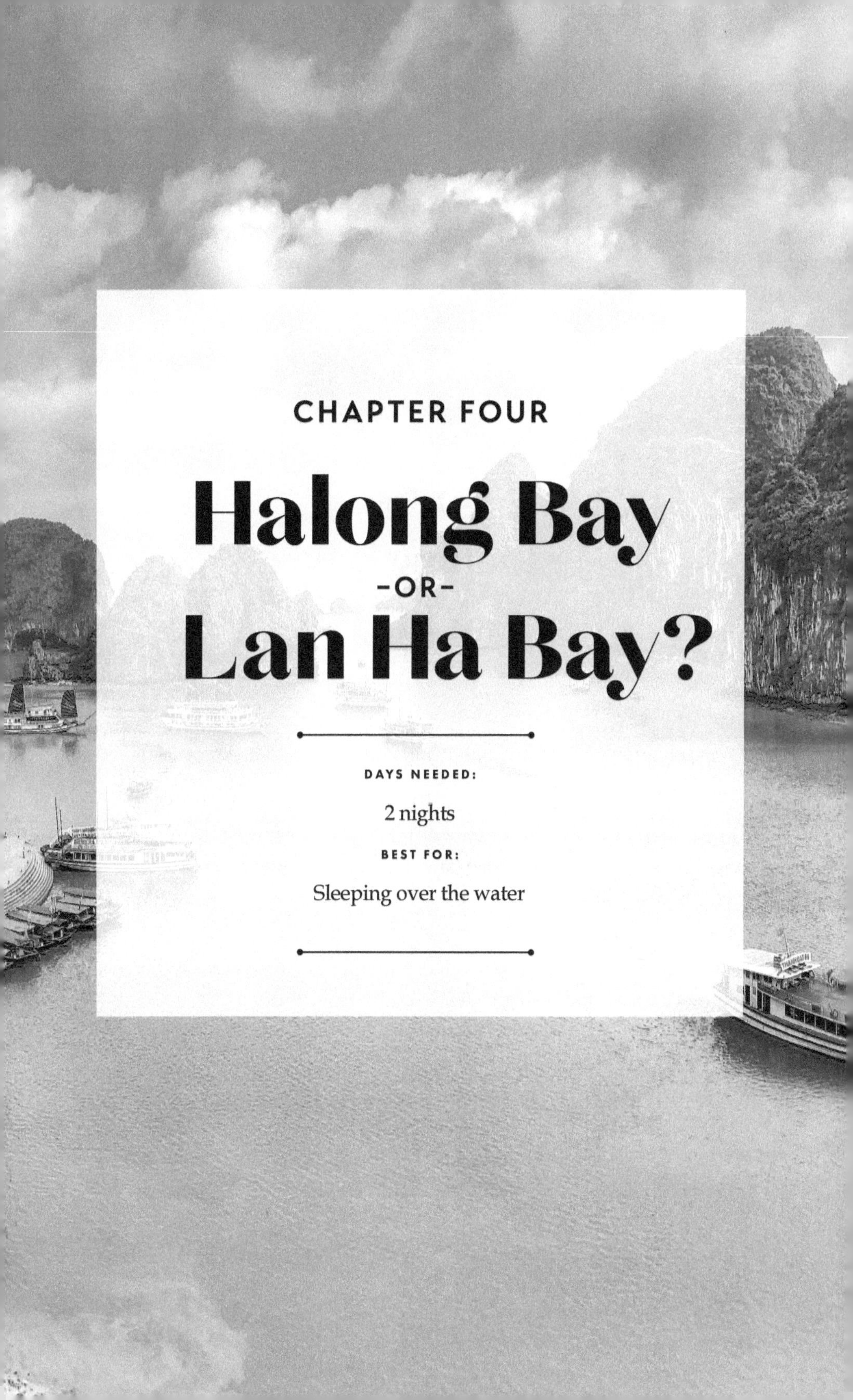

CHAPTER FOUR

Halong Bay
—OR—
Lan Ha Bay?

DAYS NEEDED:

2 nights

BEST FOR:

Sleeping over the water

CHAPTER THREE

Halong Bay *or* Lan Ha Bay?

Weird chapter title, I know. But I want you to have realistic expectations

Considered as one of the country's most popular tourist destinations, everyone knows about Ha Long Bay. 30 years ago, it was gorgeous. Today, it's crowded and a little dirty.

However, there is a bay just south of Ha Long Bay with clean water and gorgeous views, but no big boats.

So let me give you a little breakdown of what to expect so that you can make the proper choice of how to spend your time in Vietnam.

LAN HA BAY	HA LONG BAY
Pros: Absolutely stunning, clean water with little to no tourists around.	**Pros:** If boats are your thing, sailing on an all-inclusive ship for 2 nights with stunning views is pretty special.
Cons: You can either do a day cruise on the bay while staying on Cat Ba Island on a boat or sleep over on a floating raft…which I actually still think is a pro! Just don't expect big ships with VIP service.	**Cons:** When you stop to kayak or swim, you might find that the water is a little dirtier than you expected and that there are more boats within view than you'd like.

Now that you know, let me explain how to explore both…☞

FUN FACT!

During the Vietnam War, some Vietnamese leaders used a large cave in Halong Bay to serve as a safe house, shelter and a bomb-proof hospital for injured people and soldiers. It was in use until 1975 and is now open to visitors!

CHAPTER 4: HALONG BAY / LAN HA BAY

Lan Ha Bay

HOW MANY NIGHTS: 2 nights   **BEST FOR:** Kayaking and relaxing

Lan Ha Bay and Ha Long Bay are technically the same body of water surrounded by limestone cliffs, separated by an invisible district line. Ha Long Bay has tourism, whereas Lan Ha Bay has mostly fishermen.

When I stayed on Lan Ha Bay...I really stayed ON the bay. On a floating house in the middle of this bay where you see fishermen spending their days harvesting but you barely see any tourists (at least at the time of this publication)!

WHERE TO STAY IN LAN HA BAY
INNER X STAY

One of the most unique stays in Vietnam is this floating house on Airbnb. It's a simple fisherman style house with just a few rooms and free kayaks. There is no wifi. No data. Just nature, water, fisherman, a few other guests, glowing plankton in the water at night and incredible stars in the sky. Each night, for a set price, you'll enjoy a fresh seafood and veggie dinner with the other guests. They've got beer for cheap prices too. Breakfast is included but there is no lunch so bring snacks with you! Think Banh Mi in your purse and pringles in your suitcase!

Your hosts, Duc and Charles will arrange your transport from Hanoi. You'll take a bus to Cat Ba Island and from there, you'll be picked up by a water taxi (for 350k). Even the taxi boat to the floating raft feels like an exciting excursion.

When you arrive, plan to kayak, journal, read a book and jump from the dock straight into the water!

See Inner X Stay in real life - I made a little video for you here ☞

Ps. Hey, this place books up really fast so book them now!

💵 **Budget:** $
📍 **Where:** Lan Ha Bay   🌐 **Book Here:**

LAN HA FLOATING HOMESTAY

Fancier. Trendier. More…funner. Lan Ha Floating Homestay is more of a social experience than Inner x Stay that offers a very comfortable stay. There are hot showers, AC and outlets! But still, don't expect wifi! What you can expect are fabulous hosts, row boats, paddle boards, incredible seafood dinners and if you're lucky, live music. Oh and on this floating house, you have the option to get a room with a bathroom attached!

💵 **Budget:** $$$
📍 **Where:** Lan Ha Bay   🌐 **Book Here:**

XINH FLOATING HOUSE

Traveling with a group and want your own floating house? You can book all four single beds at Xinh Floating House and have a private little getaway of your own! There isn't much in terms of entertainment here besides water activities, so bring cards and download movies before you come! Or just plan on looking at the stars in silence.

💵 **Budget:** $$$
📍 **Where:** Lan Ha Bay   🌐 **Book Here:**

WHERE TO AFTER LAN HA BAY?

Ninh Binh: A bus to Ninh Binh will pick you up on Cat Ba, right where the water taxi drops you off from Lan Ha Bay.

Hanoi: Head back to Hanoi to head up north to Sapa or Ha Giang or to fly out somewhere equally exciting.

CHAPTER 4: HALONG BAY / LAN HA BAY

Halong Bay

HOW MANY NIGHTS: 2 nights

BEST FOR: Staying on a big boat with pretty views and sun tanning on the deck.

Best is experienced best on a 1 or 2-night cruise that takes you on a tour between tall cliff sides and limestone mountains that are absolutely stunning. Intermittently, the boat will dock at little bays where you can kayak and explore. Spend the rest of the days lounging on the deck with a cold beer and soaking up some sun. There are plenty of boats to choose from.

THE PARTY BOAT - *VIETNAM BACKPACKERS CRUISE*

Here are the highlights...

→ Epic Party Boat with a super social crowd

→ Sun deck where you can jump off into the water

→ Kayaking excursions

→ Cozy cabins

→ Transportation and all meals included

⊕ **Contact:** Book on VietnamBackpackersHostels.com/explore

⚠ **Beware:** There are so many copycats. Book directly from the source or with Vietnam Backpackers.

THE CLASSIER BOATS

Don't want to be surrounded by a party? You have classier options, all of which include all meals and transportation from Hanoi.

 Stellar of the Seas Cruise
THE BEST OF THE BEST

 Le Theatre Cruises
SUPER FANCY AND A BIT ROMANTIC

 Le Journey Halong Bay Cruise
MORE CASUAL AND FUN

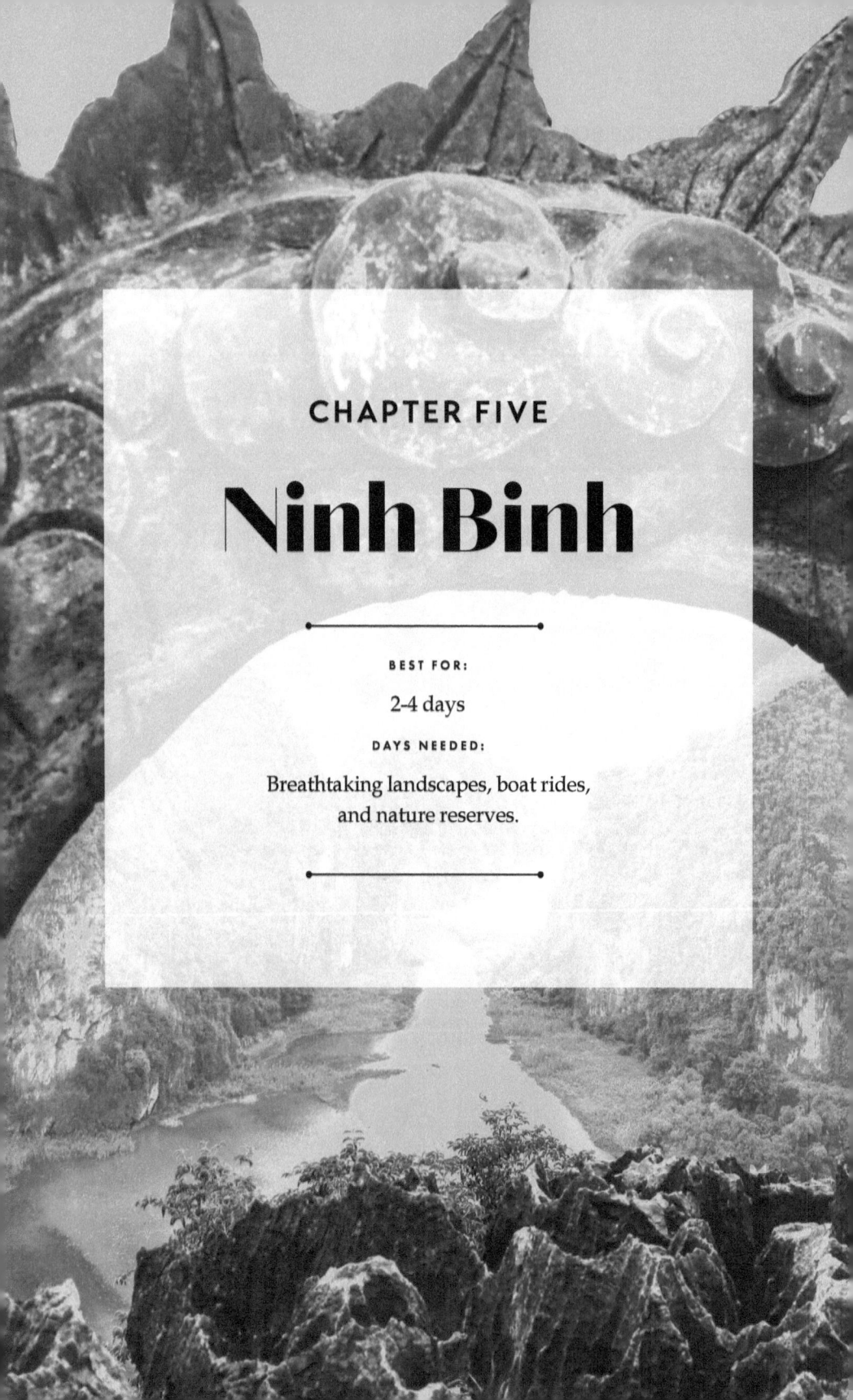

CHAPTER FIVE

Ninh Binh

BEST FOR:

2-4 days

DAYS NEEDED:

Breathtaking landscapes, boat rides, and nature reserves.

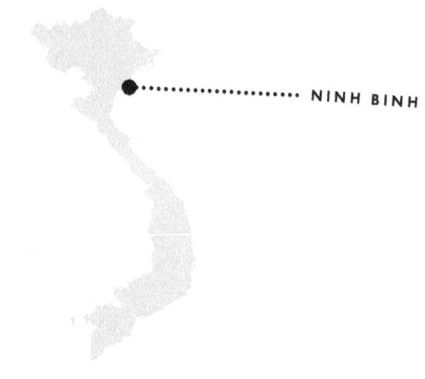
NINH BINH

CHAPTER FIVE
Ninh Binh

•—————•

You have now left Earth. Welcome to the planet of Ninh Binh.

Centuries ago, this region served as the capital of Vietnam during the Dinh and early Le dynasties. You'll be transported back in time as you explore the ancient capital of Hoa Lu, with its magnificent temples and royal ruins. These remnants tell tales of power struggles, heroic battles, and dynastic glory, immersing you in the fascinating narrative of Vietnam's past.

Somehow, days spent in Ninh Binh are equally sleepy as they are adventurous. You'll hike up a 300-step mountain just to sit in silence at the top for an hour. You'll bicycle down to the river, just to lounge in a boat pedaled through caves while sipping coffee. Here is where you come to reflect on life and walk away with a totally refreshed perspective.

FUN FACT! There are four sacred animals in Vietnam: turtles, phoenixes, dragons, and unicorns.

CHAPTER 5: NINH BINH

Areas to Know in Ninh Binh

TAM COC

A short distance from Ninh Binh city, Tam Coc is where the action is. Famous for its limestone hills and foot-pedal boat tours, Tam Coc is an ideal location to base your stay in Ninh Binh. The ancient town is the main hub for tourists visiting the area, as most of the accommodation, amenities and tours run from here. There's a large selection of restaurants, coffee places and shops selling great little souvenirs, and the town still houses loads of friendly locals with great English. There's one or two great little convenience stores here which are super useful for picking up practical things like toothpaste, snacks and toiletries if you're backpacking. **PRO TIP!** You actually don't want to stay in Ninh Binh town or city. You want to stay in Tam Coc.

BICH DONG

Around a 20-minute cycle/bike ride from Tam Coc town is Bich Dong, which is most famous for the iconic ancient pagoda. There's a really great hike up the mountain side to the pagoda which takes you through some lovely caves and has breathtaking views. There's a little path to the right of the entrance to the pagoda which leads down to an amazing little lake and up to some more caves. It's common to see some wild mountain goats here as well as hundreds, if not thousands, of dragonflies and butterflies

HANG MUA

This area is famous for the Mua Caves and Dragon Mountain, but the roads around this area are great for cycling and biking. There's so much untouched countryside, rolling rice paddies and beautiful lakes filled with lily pads to see. There isn't really a better place for a road trip, as most of the roads are relatively safe and easy to drive on, and the area is a 20 minute drive max from Tam Coc.

CHAPTER 5: NINH BINH

Where to Stay in Ninh Binh

TAM COC HORIZON BUNGALOW

Some of the best ratings for a hotel that I've ever seen, and it's easy to understand why. First, the location is nestled into the limestone cliffs but looking out on gorgeous rice fields. Second is the proximity to town. Walk, take a bicycle or rent a scooter. You are simultaneously tucked away and right next to the action. But most importantly, the hospitality here is incredible. Each guest is treated like family from the moment they arrive to the moment they leave. My favorite part about staying here was the nightly foot bath in your room before bed. Prepare to be pampered!

💸 **Budget:** $$
📍 **Where:** A lovely 10-minute stroll along rice fields into town.

🌐 **Book Here:**

NHAM VILLAGE RESORT

Waking up here feels surreal; like you're still dreaming. This is one of the most luxurious experiences you can get in Ninh Binh and is even more beautiful in person. Swim in the pool surrounded by greenery or submerge yourself in the bathtub (a luxury that can be hard to come by in this town) or indulge in a hot stone massage at the spa. Take a bicycle and adventure over to a lesser-known cave and lake called Buffalo Cave. Afterwards, come back and stroll around the property as you try to decipher, "Is this real life?" Words literally cannot serve justice to this jaw-dropping experience.

💸 **Budget:** $$$
📍 **Where:** A 10-minute drive to town (you will certainly need a scooter while staying here)

🌐 **Book Here:**

TAM COC GARDEN RESORT

A splurge you'll never forget. Tam Coc Garden Resort is an extraordinary experience of luxury and comfort amidst lush gardens and breathtaking mountain vistas. Lounge by the warm water swimming pool or book a massage at their spa. If you feel the urge to leave, there are free bicycles on site but it's a bit of a cycle into town. Better yet, don't leave at all. Spend a couple days of bliss here. When it's time to explore, book a cheaper place closer to town.

Budget: $$$
Where: 20-minute bike ride outside of town

Book Here:

TAM COC TROPICAL HOMESTAY

What makes this place really special is the location! The property's prime location places it conveniently in the heart of the town, just a short 5-minute stroll away from the Tom Coc boat tour, a quick 10-minute bike ride to the Mua caves, and approximately 30 minutes by bike to reach the Trang An area. It's got a swimming pool, free bikes and in proper Ninh Binh fashion, a host who will make sure that your every need is met from laundry to bus-ticket bookings.

Budget: $$
Where: Center of town

Book Here:

HALI HOME NINH BINH

Hostel-stayers, this is the place! You'll be staying in pristine bug-free dorms nestled in nature on a lake! By far the most beautiful budget option in Tam Coc, you'll be taken care of like you're the long-lost child of Nam, your host. You'll meet other travelers, take free bicycles to cycle into town for dinner and then come back to listen to the sounds of nature and look up at the stars. Hostel heaven.

Budget: $
Where: A lovely 15-minute bike ride into town or a 30-minute walk

Book Here:

CHAPTER 5: NINH BINH

Where to Eat in Ninh Binh

COFFEE & BREAKFAST

BRICK COFFEE SHOP

If you're looking for a classic americano or latte, head here to Brick Coffee Shop, a quaint little spot with craft coffee and pastries. They've also got coconut coffee and egg coffee. This is a lovely place to come with your laptop or journal and work or reflect. It's also on the way to the Trang An boat launch which makes it a convenient stop on your way to your adventure.

⊙ **Open:** 7am-9pm
📍 **Where:** A 10-minute walk or a 1-minute drive from Aroma Indian Restaurant

📍 **Google Maps:**

AN TAM COC RESTAURANT & COFFEE

When you're sick of fruit and eggs for breakfast, come here for a warm bowl of pho or a filling banh mi sandwich. For a more unique breakfast experience, try the Xoi Ga, a traditional sticky rice dish paired with tender shredded chicken. And no visit to this place would be complete without ordering the renowned Vietnamese Egg Coffee, a velvety combination of strong coffee and creamy whipped egg yolk that offers a filling boost of energy.

⊙ **Open:** 8am-10pm
📍 **Where:** In the center of town near the lake

📍 **Google Maps:**

LUNCH & DINNER

FAMILY RESTAURANT

I was drawn in by the duck roasting on a spit in front of their restaurant. How can you say no to that?! One of the most popular restaurants in Ninh Binh for delicious and fresh Vietnamese food! Family offers up the classic dishes such as Pho, Bun Cha and fresh spring rolls. While their prices are just a tad bit higher than what you'd expect in rural Vietnam- you can still totally afford it, even on a budget. Treat yourself to a $5 meal! And if you're not in the mood for Vietnamese, like any well-rounded restaurant, there are a few western options for picky eaters.

Open: 8am-11pm
Where: Main road in Tam Coc

CHOOKIE'S BEER GARDEN

Romantic, but not in a kissy way. This beer garden feels like a scene out of a movie with twinkly lights, little private bungalows, fireplaces and a long wading pool that reflects all the hues around it. Come cuddle up by the fire, order a craft beer and a pizza. The atmosphere is super relaxed with a mix of backpackers and families. And the staff are genuinely happy to see you and take care of you here!

Open: 8am-10pm (I recommend coming around sunset)
Where: It's a short walk towards the edge of town, on the main road, and absolutely worth the extra steps!

facebook.com/chookiesninhbinh

AROMA INDIAN RESTAURANT

When the weather gets cold, a warm bowl of Indian curry and naan bread is what you need to warm up. Right on the main drag is Aroma Indian Restaurant. I've ducked out of the cold into the restaurant quite a few times in my day, and it always hits the spot. Order a cold beer, connect to the wifi and order a thali (one tray with many menu items to try) and stick with a classic like palak paneer or butter chicken. Don't skip the garlic naan.

Open: 8am-10pm
Where: Main road in Tam Coc

 Have you joined my Solo Girls Travel Facebook Group yet?

CHAPTER 5: NINH BINH

Drinking & Nightlife in Ninh Binh

NAM COFFEE BEER GARDEN

Don't be surprised if your waiter is a child who is very excited to practice his English with you as he brings you the menus! Don't worry, his parents will quickly follow with a proud smirk on their face. They can't stop these kids from being friendly, it runs in the family! Sit down and order a beer. They might bring you some fruit, too. If it's green season, you'll be sitting at the edge of an emerald rice field. If it's harvesting season, then you might get a free farming demonstration.

⊙ **Open:** 9am - 8:30pm

♥ **Where:** Walkable from the lake, on the way to Tam Coc Horizon Bungalow

♥ **Google Maps:**

LIN CHI CRAFT BEER

Actual craft beer at affordable prices! And of course, cheap beer at cheap prices! After a long day of relaxing, this is the place to come relax more. The people watching is fabulous, the girls usually give you a little bowl of peanuts and the music is pretty damn great. All around, good vibes and great value.

⊙ **Open:** 8am - 11pm

♥ **Where:** On the main drag of town, just south of the lake

♥ **Google Maps:**

PRO TIP! The best place to visit after Vietnam is Angkor Wat in Cambodia. Get the Cambodia Guide here ☞

PARKING LOT BUS BARS

There is a parking lot (where the main buses pick up and drop off) that is home to several buses that have been converted into party buses…that don't move. It's basically a rooftop bar with music, karaoke and drink specials. How wild it gets depends on the crowd. Sometimes it's mellow, sometimes it's wild. Don't like one bus's vibe? Move to the next bus.

PRO TIP! While you're waiting for your 10pm bus pick up to head to the next city, come here a little early for a last hoorah!

◎**Open:** They start turning on their lights when the sun goes down.

📍**Where:** Look for Harbour Bus Bar on GoogleMaps

PRO TIP! If you're riding your bike around and looking for a beautiful off-the-beaten path place to take a break, Google: Bia tươi restaurant beer.

CHAPTER 5: NINH BINH

Things to Do in Ninh Binh

BOAT TOURS

Boat tours through the limestone caves and emerald green landscapes are a must when visiting Ninh Binh!

There are several boat adventures to choose from. When you check into your homestay, you'll likely be given the same map of the town with a few different boat piers to choose from. Your homestay host will likely recommend the Trang An boats… but every host recommends them which is why they get crowded. That's not to say you shouldn't consider them, but just know that you have many options beyond Trang An. My top recommendations are:

Van Long Natural Reserve: A stunning hidden gem.

Trang An: The most popular one just a 10-minute scooter ride from town.

Tam Coc: Right in town, walking distance to all the restaurants!

VAN LONG NATURAL RESERVE

You might be the only visitors when you hop in a boat here. It's 100k (plus a 50k tip to your boat driver) to cruise for two hours through the channels while listening to the sound of birds singing in the distance. It's truly amazing...yet, homestay hosts don't seem to know to recommend it.

💵 **Budget:** $
📍**Where :** 20 km north of Tam Coc. Ride your motorbike or take a taxi.

📍**Google Maps:**

TRANG AN BOAT TOUR

Just outside of Tam Coc in an area called Trang An which is a 10-minute scooter ride, a 30-minute bike ride or a quick taxi ride away. This one is so popular that it does tend to get busy with locals, especially around the holidays. So busy, in fact, that the entrance kind of looks like disneyland. Don't be too off put by this.

When you arrive, you'll be given the chance to choose your route. Choose route #1. You will then embark on a 2-3-hour tour around a labyrinth of floating pagodas, limestone caves and stunning landscapes. You get the chance to hop off the boat to explore at least 3 of the incredible ancient temples, which the locals still use for prayer.

These stopovers allow you to see the stunning biodiversity and architecture of Ninh Binh up close and personal, and the individual islands are full of wild dragonflies and birds. As the tour continues, you drift through the narrow caves, thanks to the steady hand of your tour guide. Be prepared to duck to avoid jutting stone formations and look out for bats!

Budget: $$

Where: About 10km out of town. You can ride your scooter or bike there, but don't plan to walk!

Google Maps:

TAM COC BOAT TOUR

If you don't have the time or energy to lug yourself to the other side of town, don't fret. Some people say that the Tam Coc Boat Tour is a more peaceful experience than the Trang An boat tour…and this boat tour is right in town!

Head to the boat pier in Tam Coc via bicycle, where dozens of little boats and their captains are waiting to take you on a magical ride through caves, jungle, wetlands, and mountains. You'll see locals in the water digging for clams or fishing for their family. Even more awesome, most boat captains row the entire way with their feet. It's quite the spectacle and yet, makes total sense.

The entire ride lasts about an hour; maybe more if you stop and buy some coffee or snacks from the boat vendors along the way. Just don't fall for the "buy a coffee for your captain?" trick. Your capitan shares the profit with the coffee lady.

💰 **Budget:** $

📍 **Where:** Right in town! Look for Tam Cốc-Bích Động on Google Maps

📍 **Google Maps:**

PRO TIP FOR THE BOATS! Bring cash and sunscreen!

VISIT AND HIKE THE MUA CAVES

It's only 300 steps to the top of the world! Hike up the mountain where you can see all of Ninh Binh and its rivers that look like veins running through rice fields. You can see boat tours, mountain goats, and waves of mountains in the distance. When you're done, take a right at the bottom of the stairs (as you're coming down) and venture off to find the caves. You'll walk through dark caves with watery pools below. The water is fresh, clean, and free of monsters – so feel free to take your shoes off and splash about.

📍 **Where:** Right next to Nguyen Shack

BICH DONG PAGODA

Welcome to Vietnam's biggest Buddhist temple complex! This historic pagoda complex, dating back to the 15th century, often referred to as the "Pagoda of the Jade Grotto," was constructed in three levels, resembling a breathtaking stack of natural caves ascending up the limestone cliffs. As you walk through, touch the knee of monk statues for good luck. Not only is Bich Dong easy to get to via bicycle or scooter, but it's also free! Pair this adventure with a visit to Mua Caves, conveniently located near each other.

Budget: Free
Open: 7am-5:45pm

CUC PHUONG NATIONAL PARK

A dense forest with a majestic 1000-year-old tree, prehistoric cave system, a turtle & primate conservation center, an observation tower and if you wish- go on a 2 hour hike! This national park is worth a visit but is an adventure you must commit to.

You can either drive a scooter about 60km - for the whole trip. Pack water, snacks and a flash light for the cave!

You can take a local bus which takes about 2-3 hours to get here. Again, pack snacks and water.

If you do either of these options, read this blog:

Or make it easy on yourself and go with a tour via GetYourGuide. Here's the one I recommend:

CHAPTER 5: NINH BINH

How to Get Around Ninh Binh

MOTORBIKE OR BICYCLE

By far the best way to get around in Ninh Binh is by motorbike. If you're a confident driver, there's plenty of places to rent bikes in Tam Coc for around $5 per day, and most also have bicycles (around $1.50 per day) for those that prefer to cycle. The whole of Ninh Binh is spread across 30km, so walking isn't really a great option if you want to see anything outside the main town.

When you first arrive in Ninh Binh, whether you've traveled by bus or train, it's likely that you will find yourself in Ninh Binh city - a taxi ride from Tam Coc town and most of the pagodas/attractions.

TAXI

A taxi from the outskirts of the city to Tam Coc will set you back around 150,000VND if you're using a metered one (always recommended) and more if you're paying a set price. Look out for Mai Linh taxis, as these are available all over Vietnam and are usually metered.

 Use your map to move around more easily! ☞

CHAPTER SIX

Phong Nha

BEST FOR:

2-5 days

DAYS NEEDED:

Caving adventures, biking around farmlands and relaxing on the river.

CHAPTER SIX

Phong Nha

•———————•

Want to spend the night in a cave? The vortex of nature in Phong Nha is unlike anything you've ever experienced...

Officially a UNESCO World Heritage Site, Phong Nha Ke-Bang National Park is heavily protected and preserved. Here lie millions of years of unspoiled, virgin Earth. With such preservation, it's no surprise that there are still mysteries to be discovered within this National Park. Take for example... Son Doong Cave. Son Doong Cave is the biggest cave in the world. Yes, the biggest cave in the world is right here in Vietnam. Even crazier...this cave was only accidentally discovered in 1990 by a local farmer just doing his thang. The cave was officially surveyed and measured by the The British -Vietnam Cave Expedition Team in 2009 and only opened to tourists in 2014.

However, take that cave off your bucket list unless you have $3,000 USD to spend. Instead, come explore the cave system around Phong Nha which is home to equally impressive (yet slightly smaller) caves with underground beaches next to underground rivers (yea, you heard that right). Join a trekking group for a day or spend a few nights in the caves. Or don't. Phong Nha is also a nice place just to stay on the river and relax in peace for a few days.

CHAPTER 6: PHONG NHA

How to Spend Your Time in Phong Nha

Most people arrive in Phong Nha and get a good day's rest before even thinking about going into the caves. Then they'll spend a night or two or three in the caves. They'll then return, with muddy clothes and shoes that need to be laundered, and have another rest night or two in Phong Nha along the river (the river in this town is stunning).

Now, let me be totally honest with you and tell you that I have never gone caving in Phong Nha. I am always the supportive friend that comes with the caver. I stay behind to eat and write and then welcome my friends out of the cave and listen to them gush about how their cave experience was one of the best experiences of their life. The cave experiences are always the same: surreal, challenging, rewarding, awe-inspiring, incomparable to any other adventure on earth. Really. My boyfriend went on a 3-day trek and hasn't stopped talking about it since.

But just know, that if you're not sure if you want to cave - or if you're traveling with someone who wants to cave on their own - staying back at one of these hotels to ride scooters through green farmland, take a paddle board out on the river or to have a digital nomad break and work is a joy, too.

…although, I'm now dead set on returning to Phong Nha to go caving next time I'm in Vietnam. It's my time!

EXPLORE THE CAVES

These caves and their ecosystems are super protected! In fact, each cave has a caretaker. The caretakers are cave-exploring companies responsible for keeping their caves in good health and condition. This is a brilliant way to introduce tourism to the caves while carrying a sense of responsibility for the caves! This also means that not every company has access to every cave - but the caves they do have access to, they know very well.

Since as long as I can remember, I have been a fan of one caving adventure company called Jungle Boss. They have an incredible reputation for safety and for leading incredible cave treks.

CREDIT: JUNGLEBOSS

Jungle Boss hosts a range of caving expeditions with levels varying from "very easy" to "extremely strenuous". Have a look at the tours they offer here:

If you're in doubt of which one would suit you best, reach out to them and ask! They have hosted people from all around the world with different physical capabilities and fears! They are here to guide you from beginning to end, literally.

Just throwing this out there, my boyfriend recently did the 3-day / 2-night Tiger Cave Series which included sleeping on beaches near underground rivers and he absolutely loved it. He loved getting to know the group he was with, the skilled and humorous porters that came along with him and he also said the food was pretty damn good.

One more note: My boyfriend and I met a solo traveler in Ninh Binh and my boyfriend suggested he meet us down in Phong Nha for the trek - and he did! Don't be afraid to ask other solo travelers to join you.

Packing for Caves

If you plan to go caving, pack accordingly. Here is the packing list Jungle Boss gave us for my boyfriend's 2-night expedition:

Tick as you pack! ✓

○ Two sets of long pants & long-sleeved-shirt to avoid poison ivies and mosquitoes

○ Two sets of changing clothes for the nights at basecamp

○ Swimwear

○ Two pairs of long socks

○ Small backpack

○ Sandals or flip-flops

○ Dry bag (optional)

○ Hiking shoes (optional) or you can borrow from Jungle Boss

○ Hat, sunglasses, sunscreen, insect repellent, toothpaste, toothbrush

Their porter will help you carry 3kg of gear.

…now this being said…let me tell you a funny story.

There was one german girl on my boyfriend's caving expedition. She came with long acrylic nails that she had just gotten done, leggings, and a light jacket. This girl wasn't prepared! She actually wanted to turn back at some point but the crew was supportive. She survived and thrived, despite not being perfectly packed. So do try to plan ahead but don't let the stress eat you alive.

CHAPTER 6: PHONG NHA

Where to Stay in Phong Nha

THE CAVES

Where you really want to stay is underground in a cave, but for your days before and after cave trekking, here are the places I recommend you stay.

FUNNY MONKEY

My #1 pick for where to stay in Phong Nha is Funny Monkey. Located on the river, run by women, with a cafe and laundry and amazing wifi! The women here became my big sisters. When I had a bad hotel experience down the street, I'd come here and ask for advice and help. I eventually moved hotels and stayed here for three days. I loved it so much that I am considering coming back and living here for a month! Book a riverview room if it's available!

Budget: $
Where: Main road on the river
Address:

Book Here:

JUNGLE BOSS HOMESTAY

The caving company I recommend most is Jungle Boss, and they just so happen to also have a homestay. Staying here makes sense if you're coming for the caves! It's also nice to stay in a place buzzing with cave excitement, whether it's from people about to enter the caves with excitement or explorers who have exited the caves victorious.

Budget: $
Where: Main Road
Address:

Book Here:

JUNGLE BOSS LODGE

…and Jungle Boss has this beautiful property with a pool. I swear Jungle Boss did not sponsor this book (although they totally should); they are just that great. Jungle Boss Lodge is more picturesque and romantic with rice field views that offer a little getaway from the hustle and bustle of travel life. Note that you will need a scooter to get to town!

Budget: $
Where: 2-minute scooter from town
Address:

Book Here:

PHONG NHA FARM STAY

Sunset in the pool overlooking the rice fields! The view from the outdoor pool is so surreal and the best thing about this place. With its own bar, garden, and sun terrace, it just screams 'vacation'! For all those adventurous types, I highly recommend renting a scooter and exploring the rural roads between the farmlands! And if you're in the mood for a splurge, they also have private pool villas.

Budget: $$
Where: 10-15 minute drive from the river

Book Here:

CENTRAL BACKPACKERS

This is the party hostel. Every night of the week, they have something on their social calendar whether it's beer pong or drink specials that get all the guests gathering together. The hostel has an on-site restaurant, a pool table and a beautiful pool that backs up to some cliffs. Most conveniently, however, the buses tend to drop you right in front of Central Backpackers when you're arriving from out of town. If you're in your 20's or early 30's, this is going to be a fun place for you to stay. Any older and you might feel out of place amongst the youngin's.

Budget: $
Where: On the main road, about a 15-20-minute walk from Bella Cafe.
Address:

Book Here:

Learn How to Travel Longer, Cheaper and Safer

Get The One-Way Ticket Plan, available in paperback, kindle and audio.

Get yours at Alexa-West.com ☞

CHAPTER 6: PHONG NHA

Where to Eat in Phong Nha

Listen, Phong Nha is a tiny little town. When it comes to food, the good stuff is usually right in front of your face. Here, the guest houses and hostels have mastered the art of 'yum'. But if you're really in the mood for some foodie adventures...here you go.

BELLA CAFE

Owned and on the property of Funny Monkey Homestay, Bella Cafe is where I eat most of my meals in Phong Nha. The fresh shrimp spring rolls with dipping sauce are delicious enough to order every day and are a meal in themselves. If you want to treat yourself, you can order a BBQ dinner in advance where they'll serve you freshly grilled meat and veggies - all with a stunning view of the river. Bonus: They have bubble tea!

⊙**Open:** Daily 7am - 10pm
⚲**Where:** Center of town
facebook.com/bellaCafePhongNha/

BAMBOO CHOPSTICKS

Packed every day and night with travelers! I suppose it's because the menu offers you the option to break away from rice and noodles. You can order smoothie bowls, burgers, and sandwiches! Another huge bonus is that Bamboo Chopsticks has a vegetarian menu, which can be hard to find in Vietnam! Also come here for the coffee. And live music.

⊙**Open:** Daily 7am - 1:30pm
♥**Where:** Center of town

GANESH INDIAN RESTAURANT

So good that I forgot to take a photo! I love when a restaurant has a manager walking around to welcome guests as they sit down. It makes you feel like you're coming home for dinner. I asked the manager for a recommendation and ordered the Lamb Punjabi and Butter Chicken. They did not disappoint! Plus, the garlic naan was huge! Do not hesitate to come here.

⊙**Open:** Daily 10am - 10pm
♥**Where:** Center of town
Address: Phong Nha Village

PUB WITH COLD BEER

Yes that's the name. Across rocky hills in the middle of nowhere, you'll find a great pub owned by a humble farming family. Naturally, they grow their own ingredients, so you get to experience firsthand how your food is prepared, which includes killing your own chicken. For all those concerned, you can choose not to and yes, the chicken dies humanely. This is the true farming experience. Just know that you'll need to ride a motorbike to get here! The drive is spectacular!

⊙**Open:** Daily 6am - 12am
♥**Where:** On the edge of Phong Nha-Ke Bang National Park

♥**Google Maps:**

CHAPTER 6: PHONG NHA

Things to Do in Phong Nha

LEARN TO DRIVE A SCOOTER

The roads are flat and long. You can take a bike and drive along the river on back roads past farmers and chickens and fascinating sites. I rented a scooter with my homestay, Funny Monkey, then filled up on gas, then just drove around! It's nice to have a scooter here even just because the restaurants are spread out. Don't feel like walking 10 minutes down the road to grab lunch? Just jump on your scooter…. that you totally know how to ride.

Three Tips:

☞ Tell your homestay that you need a lesson.

☞ Do not fill up on gas on the side of the road. Instead, go to the gas station but know that the lady will try to cheat you. Ask for 3 liters which should be around 70k. Confirm that price and watch to see that she does indeed put 3 liters in.

☞ Sorry, but this is the only gas station here.

Want a driving mission? Head to The Duck Stop

THE DUCK STOP

Here's the deal. There's this place amongst the farmland that is home to a huge flock of human-friendly ducks. They like to be pet and cuddled! You come here, pay 100k and not only do you get to feed the ducks but you also get to feed yourself as these prices include a rice pancake and cold drink for you! The family is so friendly and you're bound to meet other travelers while you're here. You'll be laughing and smiling the whole time. There is something about ducks that just brings out the kid in us…

🕒 **Open:** Morning to evening

🏠 **Address:** Hưng Trạch, Bố Trạch, Quảng Bình

📍 **Google Maps:**

CHAPTER 6: PHONG NHA

How to Move Around Phong Nha

MOTORBIKE

If you know how to ride a motorbike, this is a MUST. With a bike, you get access to the most off-the-grid locations, explore farm lands, and go on your own mini tours through the park. Plus, this is a great way to explore the town. Most places rent bikes for 150k.

PRO TIP! Take photos of your bike before you leave the shop. Document any existing scratches or dents. This is standard practice for South East Asian bike rentals

BICYCLE

Rent a bicycle and you can get around town very easily. You can also explore nearby rice paddies!

TAXI

You will not find many taxis here in Phong Nha. In fact, when you get dropped off at 4am in front of Central Backpackers Hostel, be prepared to walk with your gear for about 15 minutes to reach a hotel.

But like…imagine how much money a taxi could make just waiting by the bus every morning, right? #BusinessIdea

CHAPTER 6: PHONG NHA

How to Get to Phong Nha

BY AIR

A quick way to get to Phong Nha is by flying to Dong Hoi Airport (VDH), which is the nearest airport to the town. From major cities like Hanoi or Ho Chi Minh City, you can find direct flights to Dong Hoi. Once you land in Dong Hoi, you can take a taxi or arrange transportation to Phong Nha, which is about a 45-minute drive away.

BY BUS

From Ninh Binh, you can jump on an 8-10-hour sleeper train to Phong Nha that will drop you in town around 4am. Then you have to walk to your hotel. It is a true "yep, I'm a backpacker" experience.

BY TRAIN

The most scenic option and possibly the most comfortable option is the train. You can get a sleeper car, bring snacks and walk around. However, if you take the train to Dong Hoi, you will have another 45-minute taxi ride into town.

For this reason, I usually opt to take the bus to Phong Nha because it drops you directly in town!

For the most comprehensive "how to get here" - go here:

CHAPTER SEVEN

Hue

BEST FOR:

3 days/4 nights

DAYS NEEDED:

Lots of history, sipping coffees in the morning and going on food tours at night.

CHAPTER SEVEN

Hue

•————•

Vietnam, a country which was once divided with the Communist Party in the North, and the freedom fighters in the South, it is no surprise that during the conflict of the Vietnam War, Hue was literally caught in the middle...as Hue is located right in the middle of Vietnam.

The Viet Cong conquered and held Hue captive for 24 days during the Vietnam War. In attempts to further their position south, they killed anyone who was educated beyond a high school degree, and anyone who sympathized with the US. In just 24 days, 3,000 Vietnamese were killed before the US forces came to their aid.

Generally, in order to preserve ancient buildings during the Vietnam war, the US Military avoided air bombings and artillery while fighting the Vietnamese communist party- but they had to make an exception to stop the amount of violence happening in Hue and as a result, a large portion of the city was ruined- but not all.

Hue is still home to some of the most gorgeous historic sites and relics in the country. There have been massive preservation efforts, historical reconstruction, and a few lucky sites that were spared.

You only need a couple days in Hue, all of which will be spent soaking up surreal ancient history and understanding the travesties that occurred during one the most violent wars the world has ever seen. Each temple, tomb, and historical site left standing makes this city come alive with stories and secrets waiting to be discovered.

CHAPTER 7: HUE

Areas to Know in Hue

IMPERIAL CITADEL

The main attraction of Hue, home of ancient Emperors and some of the most historic sites in Vietnam.

THE IMPERIAL TOMBS

To the north of the Imperial Citadel lies the seven imperial tombs of Hue, honor of the ancient Emperors and transport you back in time to the 17th century.

THE NEW CITY

Across the bridge from the Imperial Citadel, lies the New City with modern buildings, restaurants, hotels, and nightlife.

HISTORICAL OUTSKIRTS OF TOWN

You can find even more tombs, temples, and historic bridges outside of the main attractions in Hue. If you've got a 3rd day to spare in Hue- sign up for a tour or rent a motorbike to go exploring.

CHAPTER 7: HUE

Where to Stay in Hue

PILGRIMAGE VILLAGE BOUTIQUE RESORT & SPA

Bask in a rustic and secluded resort away from the center of this bustling city. Stay in bungalows surrounded by lush gardens, villas with pool access or villas with private pools. Pilgrimage Village is the perfect place for an intimate getaway solo or with a romantic partner! Aside from their pool and spa, you can also sign up for yoga and Tai Chi classes. Don't worry about being too far from the city center, this resort offers private tours and a shuttle service into town. Then, when you're done exploring, you can come back and snuggle into nature.

Budget: $$$

Where: The resort's location is slightly outside the town center, approximately a 10-minute drive in a taxi that costs around $6 USD.

Book Here:

ROSALEEN BOUTIQUE HOTEL

Did you say pool AND sauna? Sign me up! Stay at Rosaleen where you can sunbathe next to their outdoor pool while ordering from a pool-side menu. The rooms here are spacious and luxurious- some with their own breezy balcony. One of the best things about it is that it's located at the heart of Hue and just a short distance away from popular tourist spots. Not sure where to start going? The friendly staff would help you out with that!

Budget: $$

Where: 5 minutes from the Perfume River

Book Here:

JADE SCENE HOTEL

A stay at Jade Scene Hotel places you in the heart of Hue. The hotel's central location on Hung Vuong Road, one of Hue's best shopping streets! If you're eager to explore, the 19th-century Dai Noi Imperial Palace Complex is just a 20-minute stroll away. Then come back to relax at the rooftop pool and bar. Finally, cocoon in your room equipped with a work desk, bathtub, balcony, and air conditioning!

Budget: $$
Where: Center of town

Book Here:

AMY 2 HOSTEL HUE

Arriving late? Sometimes your bus gets into Hue after midnight...and that's stressful. No problem when you book at Amy 2 – they will sort you out with their 24-hour reception. This place is quickly becoming a backpacker favorite for solo female travelers for how Amy 2 goes above and beyond for the safety of their guests. Close to the train station and bus station, this place is as convenient as it gets. They have both dorms (including female-only dorms) and private rooms for an affordable price.

Budget: $
Where: Hue Town

Book Here:

FUN FACT! The Vietnamese New Year is known as Tet and it's one of the most popular festivals in Southeast Asia. It's usually held on the same day as Chinese New Year, and it's celebrated by cleaning the house, getting together with family and friends and making offerings to the ancestors.

CHAPTER 7: HUE

Where to Eat in Hue

BUN BO HUE

Of course, your Hue food trip isn't complete without Bun Bo Hue, and this little eatery is the best place to have them. And yes, it is named after the very dish it specializes in, so don't even bother asking for directions (follow the address below). When you do find it, you'll see that it's actually a modest little restaurant packed with people. For as low as $2, you can get a generous bowl of soup with beef that just melts in your mouth. Experience eating like a local with the locals.

⊙ **Open:** Daily 5am - 7pm
Where: A few streets down the Perfume River
Address: 11B Ly Thuong Kiet

NINA'S CAFÉ

Tucked away in some obscure backstreet is a quaint family restaurant that specializes in Western, Vietnamese, and local Hue cuisine. They offer cheap dishes made with the freshest ingredients picked and caught that very day! Get a taste of the local Banh Beo and Hue Banh Khoai alongside a selection of refreshing drinks- perfect for a hot day! And don't worry, they also have a vegan and vegetarian menu!

⊙ **Open:** Daily 8am - 10:30pm
Where: A few streets down the Perfume River, near the Hung Vuong main road
♥@ninacafehuevietnam

CAFE ON THU WHEELS

Fast-food with local ingredients! Burgers, sandwiches, or rice meals, this place is all about casual dining for the active traveler! Tons of backpackers stop by here all the time to grab a quick meal or to just mingle. Here, you can share your experience with a couple of drinks and at the end of your stay, leave your mark on the walls. Don't worry! Graffiti is encouraged! It's a pretty small place- not suited for big groups - just radiating 'chill'.

◷ **Open:** Breakfast: 6am - 10:30am; Lunch & Dinner: 11:30am - 11:00pm
♥ **Where:** 500m down the Perfume River
🏠 **Address:** 3/34 Nguyen Tri Phuong Street, Hue
📘 https://www.facebook.com/cafeonthuwheelshuevietnam/

....

An Nhien Garden Vegetarian - Nhà Hàng Chay & Cafe

Up for a little drive? Go on an adventure that ends at this gorgeous fine dining restaurant surrounded by serene gardens. The food is upscale, artistically plated and using the best ingredients in the regions. Additionally, I always love a vegetarian restaurant in Vietnam because it means that I can order anything and it comes without mystery (you will soon understand what I'm talking about after being in Vietnam for a week). FYI: An Nhien Garden also offers superb cooking classes.

◷ **Open:** 7am-9pm
♥ **Where:** 10-minute drive north of the center
📘 facebook.com/annhiengardenvegetarian/

HANH RESTAURANT

Also called 'Le Hanh' or 'Quan Hanh', this traditional Vietnamese restaurant is famous in Hue! Try their Chao Tom (shrimp around sugar cane stick) & Banh Khoai (crispy fried potato cake). This place is always busy during high season which is always a great sign of a high-quality establishment. The service is on point, food comes out hot, and the beers are always cold. The perfect place for a true Vietnamese cuisine experience.

◷ **Open:** Daily 10am – 9pm
♥ **Where:** New City

CHAPTER 7: HUE

Nightlife & Fun in Hue

BROWN EYES BAR

The party ends you when you pass out; that's the rule in this bar! In a city that sleeps early, this is one of the few bars that's still alive late into the night. I mean, with a drink selection that's probably the most extensive that you'll find in Hue PLUS a dance floor and DJ, it's no surprise that Brown Eyes Bar is so popular among tourists and locals. Catch them at happy hour and get 2 drinks for the price of 1! During happy hours, you're even greeted with a free drink and snack!

Open: Daily 5pm - late
Where: 5 minutes away from the Night Market
Address: 56 Chu Van An, Hue

THE DMZ BAR

Want lots of food choices to go with your night of drinking? The DMZ offers a mix of foreign and local alcohol alongside Italian, Western, and Vietnamese cuisine. Enjoy it in their upstairs garden terrace that overlooks the Perfume River! There's also happy hour promos on the daily!

Open: Daily 5pm and 9pm
Where: By the Perfume River, Near the Hotel Century Riverside
Address: 60 Le Loi Street, Hue

SECRET LOUNGE HUE

Casual drinking without the loud music in an open-air tropical garden designed with a traditional Vietnamese spice. Secret Lounge is worth a visit. They're also got a Foosball table, a pool table, and a big ass TV to keep you entertained!

Open: Daily 7AM - 2:30AM
Where: 10-minute drive from Hue Imperial City
Address: 15/42 Nguyen Cong Tru, Hue

CHAPTER 7: HUE

Culture & Tours in Hue

Warning: This chapter is about to get historical! You can certainly take yourself on a tour with this book and GoogleMaps, or you can hire a guide to make the day much more fun.

Here are some of the best tours in town:

 5 Must-See Places in Hue

Imperial City Tour

 Hue DMZ Tour

Tombs and Pagoda Tour

CHAPTER 7: HUE

Sightseeing in Hue

TOMBS OF THE EMPERORS

Scattered near the Perfume River, you can find seven individual, uniquely designed imperial tombs made to comfort the Emperors of the Nguyen Dynasty in the afterlife. Among these, there are three that are more popular and accessible to tourists.

The Tomb of Tu Duc, which is considered the most beautiful tomb, was made for the longest reigning Emperor of his time. Because this Emperor never had a child, he had to write his epitaph himself.

The Tomb of Minh Mang is seen as the most elegant and regal one because of its architectural design. Classical Chinese style with impeccable symmetry made a structure that blends so perfectly with the landscape you'd think it was part of nature.

Taking in a mix of French and Eastern design, the Tomb of Khai Dinh is the last emperor on the list. The architecture is more complex and is perched in an ideal location with a nice view on a hill.

THIEN MU PAGODA

On top of a hill overlooking the Perfume River, you can find this iconic 7-storey pagoda. Thien Mu is the stuff of folk rhymes and literature since it's basically the oldest religious building in Vietnam. Inside, you'll find various Buddha statues, representing different stages of his life. The legend behind the name is that there was once a mysterious old lady who showed up on the hill and foretold that a Lord would pass by and build something important. Sometimes, you might even find monks praying or practicing calligraphy here.

THANH TOAN BRIDGE

'Simple yet picturesque' has to be the best way to describe this iconic Hue bridge. As you bike through the countryside, you'll find this bridge east of the Thuy Thanh Commune. It was made to facilitate transportation and communication between the two villages on each side of the canal. One of its unique traits is that it's built with architectural details that are similar to the Japanese Bridge in Hoi An. For generations, the community has always repaired and maintained their beloved bridge.

WITHIN THE IMPERIAL CITADEL

The Imperial Citadel is a walled fortress that lies at the center of Hue. It was added to the list of UNESCO's World Heritage Site in 2010 because it holds centuries of history and culture. For a thousand years, it was the center for military and political power. Stepping into the gates feels like going back in time to a place of grand and beautiful structures where emperors of Vietnam's past once walked. There's not much left of the royal palaces and structures because of years of war, but ancient architecture and relics still remains

Within the Imperial Citadel, here are the main attractions…

☆ **Hue Jungle Crevice**

This place has a pretty… morbid backstory actually. Here, the Viet Cong imprisoned 3,000 citizens and officials and, in attempts to slow down the opposition, all 3,000 citizens were pushed off cliff to their death.

☆ Forbidden Purple City

You've heard of China's Forbidden City, right? Well, this is conceptually the same thing. This citadel was made solely for the emperor and a handful of royals and servants.

☆ Trường Sanh Residence

Also called the Palace of Longevity, these buildings were built to house the Grand Empress Tu Du, mother of Emperor Tu Duc of the Nguyen Dynasty. Restoration was completed back in 2007 so now, you visit it at the northern part of the citadel.

☆ Thái Hòa Palace

Among all the structures in the citadel, the Thai Hoa palace is the most important one in every way. It's the most majestic place in all the city and its architecture has deep philosophical, cultural, historical, and artistic meaning. At the heart of it lies the Emperor's throne where the most important ceremonies and coronations happened.

☆ The Demilitarized Zone (DMZ)

Much like North Korea and South Korea created a DMZ border during the Korean War, the Vietnamese did the same during the Vietnam War. This Demilitarized Zone was the forefront for intense battles and bloodshed. It is also home to the fascinating Vinh Moc tunnels, where hundreds of people lived for 2.5 years during these battles.

IMPORTANT TO NOTE: the DMZ is about 150 km north of Hue. If you take a day trip (around $12 USD / 273 k NVD), you can go by bus which will take you on a full 6am-6pm adventure. But if you're motorbike savvy, this is a popular stop on the way from Hue as you continue up north. The DMZ is located in the town of Dong Ha. Consider spending the night there and continuing on your motorbike journey after you explore.

CHAPTER 7: HUE

More Fun Things to Do in Hue

FOOD TOURS

PRO TIP! For the best food tours - run by women - check out ilovehuetour.com! These ladies drive you around on the back of their scooters which means that you get a mini city tour on your way between eating tasty treats.

ABANDONED WATER PARK

Creepy, beautiful and apocalyptic! There will be no swimming here- just a crazy dystopian adventure. What was intended to be a large tourist attraction never picked up traction and is now just a wasteland for adventurous tourists. Nobody really knows what happened. All we know is that millions were spent…all to be forgotten after a couple of years.

Now, you can have this whole creepy park to yourself and during the rainy season...you can CAREFULLY climb the stairs up to the water slides and get dirty as you slide down these dirty tracks. It's so much fun. Just make sure you wear some comfortable hiking clothes and closed shoes for this area because it's pretty muddy and swampy.

You won't find it in a lot of itineraries or maps, so directions are more on word of mouth. Either sign up with the 'I love Hue' Tour, or go with a buddy on this one...cause ya know...abandoned stuff is creepy on your own.

PRO TIP! If you encounter a security guard, just pay him 20k and he'll let you through.

♥Google Maps:

BACH MA NATIONAL PARK

Staying in Hue gives you access to this incredible national park. Part of the Annamite Mountain Range and the wettest region in Vietnam, Bach Ma National Park is the place to go if you want to get off the beaten path. A paradise for nature lovers, there's plenty to see including wildlife, lagoons and waterfalls. Adventurers can enjoy climbing, camping and hiking, most notably, the Summit Hike. The park is about 55 km from Hue and you have a few options to get there. Rent a motorbike, drive yourself 1 hour there or go on a trekking tour!

Here's the tour I recommend:

KAWARA MY AN ONSEN RESORT

Thinking of going to Hue in the summer? Beat the heat at this resort! You don't have to be a guest to soak here. Just show up and heal. The mineral water is said to have therapeutic qualities then detox in the sauna.

♥Where: A 20-min drive northeast of the city
🌐 kawaramyanresort.com/en/kourai-spa/   **♥Google Maps:**

MARBLE MOUNTAIN

On the Son Tra Peninsula of Da Nang lies the Indiana Jones style Marble Mountains that look more like a cluster of skyscrapers than rock formations. There are 5 mini "mountains'' in total, made of marble and limestone. On your Marble Mountain adventure, you can explore mysterious caves tucked into the mountains and visit the 220-foot-high marble Bodhisattva statue resting in the Ling Ung Buddhist Pagoda.

At the base of Marble Mountain is Non Nuoc Stone Carving Village, a centuries-old craft village here with impressive stone carved statues of Buddhist figures, dragons, and more

IMPORTANT: The very best way to explore marble mountain is to get a private driver or join a motorbike tour that takes you to Marble Mountain on the way to Da Nang or Hoi An like this:

DRIVE THE HAI VAN PASS

Headed to Hoi An or Da Nang next? Consider making an adventure out of it.

There is a very popular stretch of coastal highway starting in Hue stretching to Da Nang and Hoi An that is a popular drive for those who want to experience a motorbike adventure but don't want to traverse the whole damn country on 2 wheels. This highway stretch is called the Hai Van Pass.

You can sign up for a tour, where you'll have a guide that leads the way from Hue to Danang, or Hoi An. You can also opt to ride on the back of their bike while you take in the views. You'll stop by waterfalls and do some little hikes along the way!

The entire journey is 165 km which can be completed in 1-3 days…depending on how many stops you want to make.

Know that you can do this journey in 4 different sequences:

→ Hoi An to Hue

→ Da Nang to Hue

→ Or flip those two around and go the other direction.

→ Just ask around in Hue, Hoi An, or Da Nang and you can find this tour being offered!

Here is a 1-day Hue-Da Nang - Hoi An tour with guide ☞

DON'T WANT TO MOTORBIKE IT?

Transfer from Hue to your next hotel in style with a vintage US Army Jeep. Turn your transfer into an adventure with the wind in your hair!

Your driver will even take you to see Marble Mountain and a few other stops along the way - dropping you at your final destination in Da Nang or Hoi An.

Book here ☞

FUN VIETNAM FACT!

Vietnam is the world's largest exporter of black pepper.

CHAPTER 7: HUE

Markets & Shopping in Hue

DONG BA MARKET

More than a place for tourists to get cheap goods, Dong Ba Market is kind of like the heart and center of Hue. It's the biggest and oldest market that stretches from the Trang Tien Bridge to Gia Hoi Bridge. Hundreds of people go here to make a living or buy goods for their everyday lives. You can find anything here: food, souvenirs, and even cultural gifts that you can't find anywhere else. Make sure to keep a good eye on your stuff, though, as pickpockets are just lurking around. Also, don't forget to bargain, bargain, bargain!

Open: Daily 6am - 8pm
Address: Tran Hung Dao street, Hue

HUE WALKING STREET

Take a break from all the fast-paced touring and unwind in the new and improved Walking Street. You're now greeted with better pavements and beautiful scenery! They've even made it so that no vehicles would pass by on weekends and holidays. If you're lucky, you can catch street performances and festivals on this street.

Open: All day - Every day
Address: Nguyen Dinh Chieu

CHAPTER 7: HUE

How to Get Around Hue

TAXI

Taxis are usually more reliable in their fees, but make sure you keep watch on that meter! It starts at 15k VND for the first 2 kilometers and goes up 11,500 VND per kilometer. It's best to ask your hotel about the estimated fee, so you'll have an idea of how much you should be paying.

MOTORBIKE

Whether you're touring within town or in the countryside, motorcycles are the most ideal way to get around. Fast and accessible, hotels and restaurants all around Hue offer motorcycle rentals and even tours for as low as $10 / 228k.

BICYCLE

For a quick ride within the city, bicycles are the way to go! You can easily go through all those small alleys and inner streets to get to those hidden restaurants. There are tons of bike shops and tours that rent a bike for at least $2 a day.

CYCLO

Where there are tourists, there are cyclo drivers. It's actually a fun and unique way to get around! Sure, it's not as fast and traffic is bad, but sitting in your own little covered chair as someone pushes you to your destination is an experience in itself. You can choose to go on cyclo tours or find one walking around offering rides. Be careful when you're around an empty street at night, though. Make sure you ask for their price before picking one as some tend to up the cost for obvious tourists. For cyclos, it would usually cost roughly $5 /114k for an hour's trip. Of course, the price is less if it's just one nearby stop. Also, bring a notepad with you to write down prices as miscommunication tends to happen sometimes.

CHAPTER 7: HUE

Scams Particularly in Hue

⚠ BUS TICKET SCAMS

When it comes to booking a bus to HCMC, shop around! Hotels and tourism offices often try to increase the price to keep the difference. Let them know you're shopping around and don't be afraid to walk away. The price will magically drop. Bus tickets to HCMC should be around $20-$30.

Avoid 'Adin's Café Booking Office' and 'Moon Travel'. They are infamous for jacking up prices – no matter how friendly they may seem…

⚠ RECOMMENDATIONS FROM YOUR HOTEL

Everyone is trying to make a dime in Hue- including hotel receptionists. Be weary when you ask for massage, tour, or restaurant recommendations from your hotel. Everyone is looking to make a little commission and might give you a less-than-amazing recommendation. Good thing you have this book, ya?

⚠ ORDERING FOOD AT THE MARKET

When you order your meal…only eat when you've specifically ordered. The vendors can be tricky and bring you an extra plate of food. If you eat it…you buy it.

WHERE TO AFTER HUE?

Answer: Hoi An. I'll tell you how to get here in the "How to Get to Hoi An" in Chapter 9 on page 210.

Most people that come to Hoi An don't realize that Hoi An is home to two worlds! You've got the Ancient City and you've gone to the beach. Separated by one long road lined with rice fields, you can easily ride a bicycle and motorbike between them…but I just prefer to keep my exploring life and my beach life separate.

When I visit Hoi An, I spend a few nights in the Ancient City and a few nights at the beach. You feel like you've completely moved towns without going far.

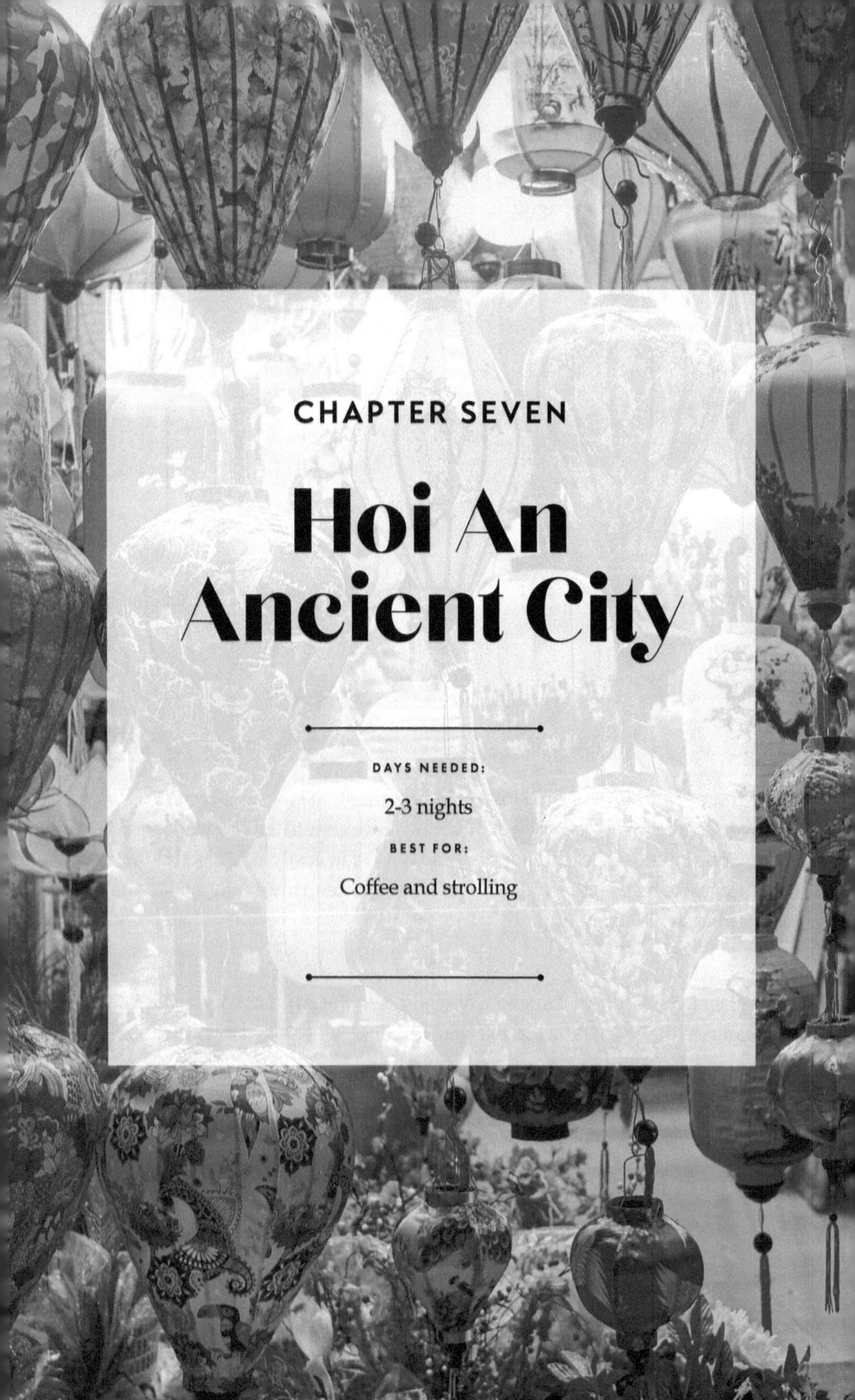

CHAPTER SEVEN

Hoi An Ancient City

DAYS NEEDED:

2-3 nights

BEST FOR:

Coffee and strolling

HOI AN ANCIENT CITY

CHAPTER EIGHT

Hoi An Ancient City

•—————•

Hoi An is magic. You'll see it and feel it the moment you arrive, and it will leave a dreamlike imprint on your mind even after you leave.

Hoi An used to be the happening spot for traders back in the day. Picture this: Chinese, Japanese, Dutch, and Indian merchants, all colliding in this little fishing town to make deals. This ancient city is located in the middle of Vietnam and holds over 2,000 years of history, which have been preserved to an impressive standard. Hoi An is incredibly picturesque with winding alleys between bright yellow French style buildings that look like illustrations come to life. The incredible ancient French architecture can be seen all over Hoi An- perfectly preserved with historical buildings turned into coffee shops and Bahn Mi stalls. The town glitters with brightly painted window shutters and rusty red tiled roofs- all begging to be photographed. By day, the town is full of bicyclists and coffee shops. By night, the entire town lights up with colorful lanterns hanging from lamp posts or floating in the river canal. This place is magical. Truly, sincerely magical

Oh, and here's a tip: if you're lucky enough to be in Hoi An during a full moon, you're in for a real treat! Once a month, the city hosts Hoi An Lantern Festival with lanterns everywhere, traditional performances, and a vibe that'll give you goosebumps. Google the exact dates while planning your visit.

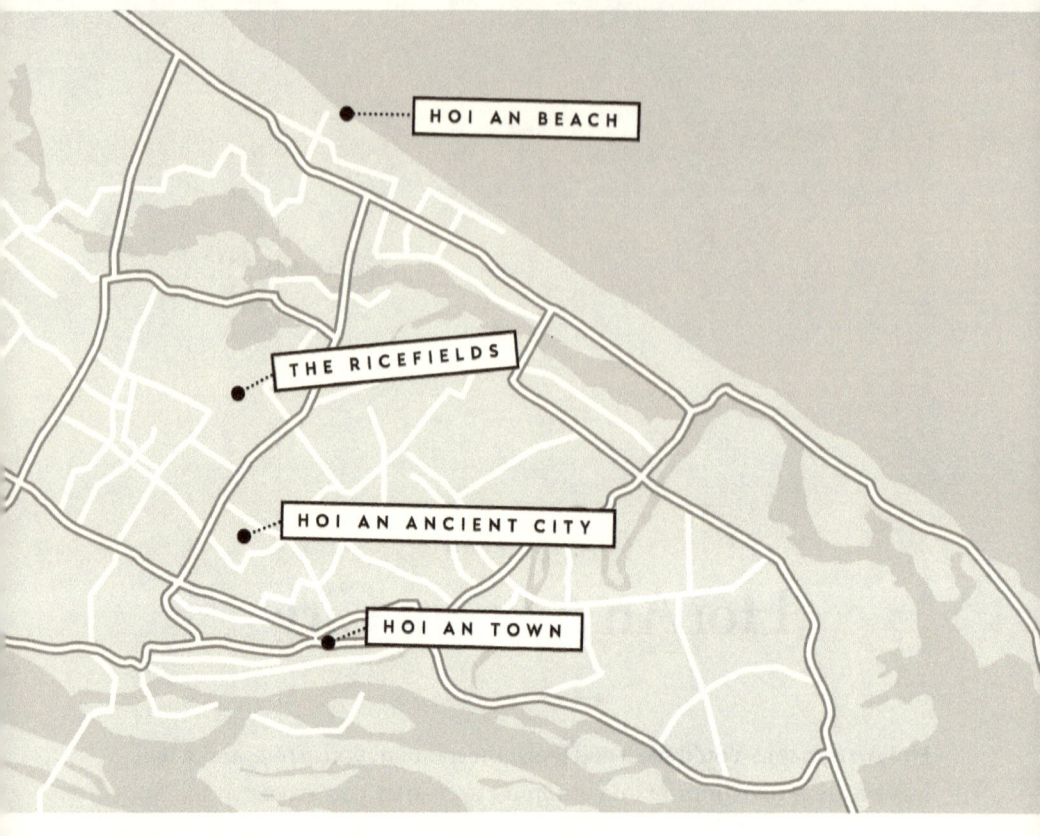

CHAPTER 8: HOI AN ANCIENT CITY

Areas to Know in Hoi An Ancient City

ANCIENT CITY

Come admire the beautiful heritage buildings dating back to the 16th and 17th century. This well-preserved town's architecture includes a mix of Chinese, Japanese, Vietnam and French colonial designed buildings. Grab something traditional to eat as you wander the streets of Hoi An at night, admiring the history and small beautifully decorated tourist shops, governed by locals with friendly smiles on their faces. One will not fail to notice the traditional lanterns which light up the streets, providing a very colorful and magical experience.

HOI AN TOWN

As you make your way away from the water, but before you come to the rice fields, there is a little pocket of town that feels more local but still scattered with quaint guesthouses, amazing massage parlors, and delicious food. For those who feel that the Ancient City is too populated with travelers and hawkers, staying in Hoi An Town might be a better option, just a 10-minute bike ride away.

THE RICE FIELDS

Bright green rice fields line the main road that connects the beach to the ancient town. With little cement paths that wind in-between bright green pastures, this makes for a surreal adventure. You'll pass herds of cattle, farmers, locals, and the famous 'old man posing with a water buffalo for $1. Don't be afraid to pedal past the fields and into the neighborhoods for a sneaky peak of local life.

FUN VIETNAM FACT

Vietnam is officially a "Tropical Country".

CHAPTER 8: HOI AN ANCIENT CITY

Where to Stay in Hoi An Ancient City

I'm going to be honest with you. It's hard to find a bad hotel in Hoi An. The culture of treating your guests like family is strong here! You will always have someone looking out for you but here are some recommendations to get your search started.

LA SIESTA HOI AN RESORT & SPA

Time to be a queen, queen. This luxurious resort features a beautiful outdoor swimming pool, a spa, and an on-site restaurant making you feel pampered and at peace! The staff go above and beyond to cater to your every need. This place feels like a Four Seasons Resort but without the wild price tag. When it's time for a stroll, you're a short walk from the old town and all the best restaurants!

Budget: $$$

Where: 13-minute walk to the Japanese Covered Bridge

Book Here:

SUNSHINE HOTEL

I planned to stay at Sunshine Hotel for 2 nights…but I accidentally stayed for 1 month. I'm not kidding. The breakfast buffet is incredible, the pool is gorgeous with full sun for tanning and your room is cleaned every day! Not to mention, the balcony with views of bright green rice paddies in the distance is the perfect way to start your day.

Located smack dab between the beach and Old Town, you've got easy access to every single area worth visiting in Hoi An. Take a free bicycle for a spin and explore. Go right on the main road and you'll ride through bright green rice fields; go left and you're 5 minutes from the city center. Sunshine Hotel also offers free shuttles to the beach and Old Town all day long. This place is THE BEST value for money and is a fabulous way to see and do it all!

Budget: $$
Where: Hoi An Town - 15-minute bike ride to the river

Book Here:

VINCENT'S HOUSE

My top pick for staying in Hoi An is also quite affordable. Staying at Vincent's House (sometimes called Vinci Villas) feels like staying at a friend's house…a friend that has a big warm pool, free bikes and daily housekeeping. Even before we arrived, Vincent was going out of his way to make sure we were comfortable, even meeting us at the bus! Breakfast is made by mama every morning. I highly recommend a cheese omelet or banana pancakes (some of the best you'll have in Vietnam). The location is about a 15-minute walk from the river, but a two minute walk from the best restaurants (Minh's Sushi and Mien Hien Vegetarian) and surrounded by affordable massage spots.

Budget: $$
Where: Hoi An Town

Book Here:

GREEN RIVERSIDE OASIS VILLA

Located on the river kind of between the beach and the city, Green Riverside Oasis makes both areas easy to explore with their free bicycles! This place is really bright and vibrant with yellow walls, bright green palm trees and a glowing blue pool. I highly recommend booking a room with a river view where you can sit on your balcony and enjoy a cup of coffee in the mornings as you watch the boats go by. I am calm just thinking about this place…

Budget: $
Where: 15-minute bike right to Hoi An Night Market

Book Here:

....

CHEERFUL HOI AN HOSTEL

Free breakfast, food tours, and friends in a clean hostel run by the most loving local woman ever. This is the authentic backpacker experience you've been longing for! If you're homesick, come here. If you're lonely, come here. If you want to experience true Vietnamese hospitality, come here! This place is oh-so female friendly!

Budget: $
Where: Right between Old Town and the beach

Book Here:

FUN VIETNAM FACT!

Vietnam is the world's second largest producer of coffee, right behind Brazil.

And talking about coffee, let me tell you where you're going to find the best in Hoi An Ancient City. On to the next page ☞

CHAPTER 8: HOI AN ANCIENT CITY

Where to Eat in Hoi An Ancient City

BREAKFAST & COFFEE

PORT CITY BAGEL & DELI

You know when you take a bite of something and have to close your eyes because it's just so delicious? That's what happened to me at Port City Bagels with their breakfast bagel sandwiches. Situated in the heart of Old Town, this is the perfect place to grab breakfast or brunch before an afternoon of exploring. Need caffeine? Owned by a Seattle couple using Vietnamese beans, you know the coffee is going to be incredible, too.

☉**Open:** Daily 8am-4pm (except Wednesdays)
📍**Where:** 6-minute walk to the Japanese Covered Bridge

HOI AN ROASTERY

The OG of coffee in Hoi An, Hoi An Roastery is an iconic coffee experience you'll never forget- I mean it. Nestled at the bottom of Hai

Ba Trung Street, it's hard to miss this gem. Staring at bright yellow walls and old shuttered windows, it feels as if you've gone back in time just to enjoy the perfect cup of coffee. Don't forget to grab a bag of beans to take home.

Open: Daily 7am-10pm
Where: Ancient City

HOME COFFEE

Come get your caffeine fix at this 3-story breezy coffee spot with a patio and gardens, both indoor and outdoor spaces and the cheapest Americano I've found! 25k VND! Home Coffee is located in Hoi An Town on your way out of the ancient city towards the beach and feels much more local than any other coffee shop I've found.

Open: Daily 6am-10pm
Where: Ancient City

REACHING OUT TEA HOUSE

When you first visit Reach Out Tea House, you'd notice nothing out of the ordinary. It's quaint, it's cute, and it has a great selection of drinks and munchies. However, when you order, you'll notice the staff are all hearing impaired. Order by writing on paper what you'd like and viola. Besides serving a wonderful cause to provide work opportunities to the hearing impaired, Reach Out Tea also has some of the best local teas and blends in the city. Win-win.

Open: Monday-Friday 8:30am-9pm/Saturday-Sunday 10am-8pm
Where: Ancient City

ROSIES CAFE

When I walked into this place, I thought I was in Bali. This is a very trendy spot with Instagram vibes and a big menu that caters to all palettes. They've got comfort food like big breakfasts with sausage and eggs. They got the healthy stuff like fig salads and nutritious smoothies. And they've also got great coffee. Rosies is a lot more expensive than the local places. You're paying around 70-110k for a meal rather than 50k for a meal, but it's quite filling and if you've got your laptop with you, this is a good place to get some work done.

Open: 8am-4pm (closed Sundays)
Where: Hoi An Town

9 GRAINS

Finally! A cafe with an enclosed, air conditioned place where I can bring my laptop to escape the heat, do some work and sip on a strong latte without sweating my butt off. 9 Grains has some of the best bread and pastries in town! You can watch them making their treats behind the scenes! I recommend ordering the ham and cheese croissant. If you're on your way to the beach, stop and grab some croissants to take with you.

⏲ **Open:** 7am-4pm
📍 **Where:** Hoi An Town

LUNCH & DINNER

STREET FOOD IN THE ANCIENT CITY & NIGHT MARKET

Since the beginning of time, women have been selling snacks on the street in Hoi An. Each vendor has a specialty from banh mi to chicken & rice to fried seafood. These dishes tend to be super cheap. You can grab and go, take a seat on the sidewalk, or pull up a plastic chair. You can find this all day all over the city… but the real streetfood spectacular is the Night Market.

Cross the bridge, over the lantern speckled water, and head towards the Night Market. Be sure to walk all the way to the end. It gets less crowded the further you go.

....

BANH MI PHUONG

2-minutes of airtime on Anthony Bourdain's episode of 'No Reservations' back in 2012 was enough to put Banh Mi Phuong on the map for all of eternity. There is so much hype around this little hole in the wall with lines literally out the door all day every day…that it's enough to roll your eyes at if you've never tried it.

Like, how good can a sandwich actually be? But I'm telling you, one bite and your world will be changed forever. I can confirm- this is the BEST BANH MI in all of Vietnam. Even better…they've never changed their prices. You pay 25k Dong for a mind-blowing Grilled Chicken Banh Mi (which I insist you try).

⏲ **Open:** Sunday-Friday 6:30am-9:30pm / Saturday 7am-9:30pm
📍 **Where:** Old Town
🏠 **Address:** 2B Phan Chau Trinh

TRUC CAFE 17 BACH DANG

You'd never know it by the looks of the storefront, but head into this tiny hole-in-the-wall to the back where you'll find riverfront seating. Then, order a super authentic bowl of Cao Lau noodles, a cold beer and enjoy watching the boats go by.

Open: All day every day
Where: Riverside in Old Town
Address: 17 Bạch Đằng, Cẩm Châu

MIN'S SUSHI BAR

Sit at the bar. I often just pop in here order some nigiri or a hand roll as an appetizer, along with a beer while watching the sushi chef masterfully prepare beautiful dishes - then head out for dinner number two. But if you're really going for it, this place has incredible sushi rolls. You can't go wrong!

Ps. There are two locations. One in old town and one in uptown near Vincent's House. I've only visited the one near Vincent's House.

Open: Daily 4pm-10pm (also, Friday-Sunday 10:30am - 1:30pm)
Where: Uptown near Vincent's House

HERBAL PIZZA RESTAURANT

I'm not going to lie...I didn't expect this pizza to be that good. Don't be fooled by the quirky decor, this pizza is legit wood-fired pizza. Order a large pepperoni pizza with olives. Good pizza doesn't need to be fancy. Oh a pro tip, on a hot day, sit inside! The air conditioning is a welcome reprieve.

Open: 11am-10pm (closed Sundays)
Where: Ancient City

MORNING GLORY (ORIGINAL)

Such a romantic spot! Famous for its traditional Vietnamese cuisine, Morning Glory offers a variety of dishes that encapsulate the essence of the region. The Cao Lau, a regional Vietnamese dish made with noodles, pork, and local greens, is a must-try. Another highlight from their menu is the White Rose dumplings - a Hoi An specialty. Lastly, as the name suggests, don't miss out on their namesake dish, the "Morning Glory" sautéed in garlic. Pro Tip: if you can, sit on the balcony upstairs where you can look down on Hoi An coming alive at night.

Open: 11am-10pm
Where: Ancient City

MINH HIỀN VEGETARIAN RESTAURANT

I have been known to eat lunch and dinner here. I'm addicted even though I'm not a vegetarian. Family-owned and affordable, what started as a small local restaurant many years ago steadily picked up popularity amongst Westerners over the years.

My favorite dishes to order are the sauteed noodle with turmeric and chive, the green banana salad, the sautéed Hoi An special noodle (cao lau), the sautéed pumpkin with roasted peanuts, and the grilled eggplant with lemongrass. They got tons of fresh juices and smoothies as well...all for extremely reasonable prices.

Open: Daily noon-10pm
Where: Northern Old Town in a small alley off of Hai Ba Trung Street
Address: 30A Dinh Tien Hoang

7 BRIDGES TAP ROOM
Date Spot Alert!

Chicago-style pizza and craft beer, anyone? Sit at the bar and chat with a bartender or find a candle-lit table in the back garden under the trees. Walk slowly through 7 Bridges so you can gaze around at the colorful walls, beautiful architecture and charming touches.

Open: Daily 11am-midnight
Where: Ancient Town

CHAPTER 8: HOI AN ANCIENT CITY

Drinking & Nightlife in Hoi An Ancient City

Outside of hostel parties, there is only elements to nightlife in Hoi An...

HOI AN NIGHT MARKET

The Night Market is the perfect place to grab a walking beer and start your night. Do some buzzed shopping with lanterns and jewelry. Eat some fresh mango roti made right in front of you. Or sit down at a plastic table and people watch as you sip $1 beers.

BARS ALONG THE RIVER

Just skip away is the boardwalk along the river, lined with bars of all kinds. There are bars with live music, bars with a rasta vibe, bars for the younger travelers to mingle and do shots...have a wander and pick a bar that suits your fancy.

WOOP WOOP BAR

What feels like a backyard party is technically a backyard party. This bar is tucked away in the winding alleys of Hoi An Town near Vincent's House. It's the place to meet other travelers and locals. I love that there is an actual bar top with stools where you can go as a solo girl, sit without feeling awkward and easily interact with people around you!

⊙**Open:** 5pm - 1am

CHAPTER 8: HOI AN ANCIENT CITY

Things to Do & See in Hoi An Ancient City

JAPANESE COVERED BRIDGE

While remaining one of the most iconic sights of Hoi An tourism, the Japanese Covered Bridge, or "Chùa Cầu" in Vietnamese, is actually a product of Japanese merchants who sought easier means of trade with surrounding communities. Although Constructed in the 17th century, the Earthquake-proof bridge still displays many of the ornate details of its time. The warm waters of the Thu Bon River flow beautifully beneath the bridge, allowing many photo ops to be had showcasing the artwork of an ancient culture. Adorned with a sacred pagoda, the Japanese Covered Bridge is said to dedicate this space for a guardian who will bless the people with happiness and well-being. A timeless must-see!

Budget: $5 USD/ 120,000 VND
Where: At the end of Tran Phu Street in Hoi-An, Vietnam
Address: Nguyễn Thị Minh Khai, Phường Minh An

FUKIAN ASSEMBLY HALL (PHUC KIEN)

A visit to Vietnam is incomplete without experiencing the spectacular Fukian Assembly Hall (Phuc Kien) located in Hoi An's Ancient Town.

In 1697, ethnic traders coming from China settled in Hoi An and established this largest and most intricate architectural Chinese Assembly hall. Avoid the street chaos and take a moment to admire the Buddhist Iconography and classic architecture. Throughout the hall, there are statues, bronze bells, horizontal lacquered boards having Chinese characters and bronze drums. It's exciting to see a very large and impressive dragon statue made of porcelain tiles affixed at the back side of the Hall.

Bonus: Nowadays Fukien Assembly Hall is more popular for amazing activities and events for celebrating Chinese festivals.

Budget: 120,000 VND (approx. 5 USD)
Open: Daily from 08.00AM to 05.00PM
Where: Old Quarter
Address: 46 Tran Phu, Phuong Minh An

BICYCLE THROUGH THE TOWN AND FARMLANDS

Hop on your bicycle and take the scenic ride through the farmlands in the opposite direction of tourists! Your destination? A farmers house. A farmer who will service you tea and be so excited that you came all the way out here to see him. This is what travel is about. Cross-cultural connections with the most unexpected friends. This is an easy day, a cheap day, and an unforgettable day.

A great destination for a bicycle ride is Coffee Quoc Cuong with a stop at Hidden Cafe Eco Farm.

COCONUT BASKET BOAT TOUR

When in Hoi An, experience life as locals do. Learn from the locals how to paddle a wooden boat through narrow streams lined with palm trees and catch little crabs without falling from the boat. Sounds simple enough? Guess again!

Ps. You may have seen these spinning boats on Instagram. If not, you'll see it there. If you want a spinning experience, bring a 100,000k tip. It takes a lot of muscle!

I recommend this tour ☞

Or pair your basket boat tour with a market tour and cooking class ☞

LANTERNS IN THE CANAL

When the sun goes down, head towards the canal where you'll find women selling bright lanterns. You light a candle and realize it into the water while making a wish. Even if you don't participate, it's quite the sight to see; a canal full of brightly colored lanterns glowing in the darkness. Prices vary from lady to lady but the average is 150,000 VND for a boat with 1-3 people. Ask around to find the best price or the nicest

FUN VIETNAM FACT!

Vietnam's unemployment rate is one of the lowest among all developing countries.

CHAPTER 8: HOI AN ANCIENT CITY

Markets & Shopping in Hoi An Ancient City

HAVE A CLOTHING MADE

Hoi An is the mecca for tailored clothing. See a dress you like? Or a playsuit that you have to have? Literally every shop will tailor that exact piece just for you- sometimes within 2 hours. They've got all the fabrics you need!

Have a particular design in mind? There are tons of tailors who are eager to make it for you...but that's the tricky part.

Pro Dressmaking Tips

→ The tailors in Hoi An are hustlers. They will never tell you 'no'. Some tailors are patient and will work with you to customize your dream dress.... and some tailors want to slap something together and hurry your ass out of town, so they can keep your money.

→ Remember that these women are tailors, not designers. Keep your concepts simple. Instead of complicated designs, choose wild fabrics.

→ Make sure to allot three days in Hoi An in case you need to return to the shop for adjustments (which you almost certainly will).

☆ **Highly Recommended Tailor:** Shine Tailor Hoi An
 www.facebook.com/shinetailorhoian/

CHAPTER 8: HOI AN ANCIENT CITY

Beauty & Wellness in Hoi An Ancient City

BLUE GIFT SPA

The best experience! I felt like a princess! So many treats and surprises and the massage was heavenly! She focused on my knots and tension! Incredible! Pro Tip: If you show up, you might be able to haggle a deal on the prices that are listed on the spa menu out front. I got quite the discount just by asking… but then I tipped generously. These women deserve your business. Do what you can afford.

Open: 8:30am - 10:30pm
Where: Hoi An Town
See services here: hoianbluegiftspa.com

RELAXY FOOT AND BODY CARE

Right across from 7 Bridges Tap Room, come get a foot massage and then head to your beer and pizza dinner. Or come for a full-body pamper session then get a pedicure while you sip herbal tea. Better yet, do both. If you're located near by Relaxy, odds are that you will keep coming back not only for the amazing treatments but also for the owners who love spoiling their guests.

Open: 9am-10pm
Where: Ancient City

LOTUS NAIL & SPA

Now is the time to play with your nails! Sparkles, clouds, flowers...or just really pretty gel. Lotus Nail is THE spot to go in Hoi An for incredible manicures and pedicures. This place can get busy so it's best that you write beforehand to make an appointment. Prices vary depending on what you want but I can tell you that you will be happy with the price.

Open: 8:30am - 8:30pm
Where: Ancient City
https://www.facebook.com/profile.php?id=100064026365873

TRAVEL NOTES:

Hey! Want to teach English abroad? You'll meet many English teachers in Vietnam. Visit Alexa-West.com/Travel-Paths for more info.

CHAPTER 8: HOI AN ANCIENT CITY

How to Get Around Hoi An Ancient City

BICYCLE

Bikes are the way to go in Hoi An! The streets are mellow and drivers are constantly cautious of the dozens of bicyclists that surround them at any given time. You can bike through the entire ancient city and down to the beach within 1 hour- taking your time for snacks, fresh coconuts and rice fields along the way.

Ps. Hoi an is so safe. You don't even need to chain your bicycle up when you park.

WALK

Hoi An is a walking city! Winding alleys and little bridges are best when you just walk and get lost amongst it all. Sidewalks are **safe** and street crossings are respected by drivers here (a rare thing for Vietnam).

MOTORBIKE

Rent a motorbike and get even further off the beaten path. Explore neighborhoods, islands, deeper into the rice fields and go all around the beach roads. Motorbikes aren't great for the Ancient City as there is so much foot traffic, but everywhere else is an open road!

GRAB TAXI

At night, opt for a grab taxi that will cost you no more than $2-3 to get anywhere in the city.

CHAPTER NINE

Hoi An Beach

BEST FOR:

2-3 days

DAYS NEEDED:

Chilling by the beach and day-drinking

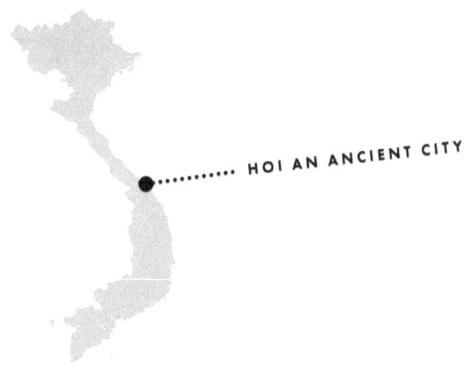

CHAPTER NINE

Hoi An Beach

———•———

The beaches of Hoi An were originally a popular trading port in the 15th century, bustling with merchants from across the globe. As the centuries passed, the traders were replaced by fishermen, their colorful boats dotting the coastline. It wasn't until the late 20th century that the beach's potential as a tourist destination was recognized. Today, Hoi An Beach is renowned for its serene beauty, water sports, and seafood delicacies, but beneath its tranquil surface, you can still catch whispers of its lively past. Just walk onto the sand in the morning and you'll see fishermen coming back in with their morning catch.

The best time to visit Hoi An Beach: During the dry season, which falls between February and August. During this period, you can expect sunny weather and pleasant temperatures, ideal for sunbathing and swimming. September to January may bring heavy showers and strong waves.

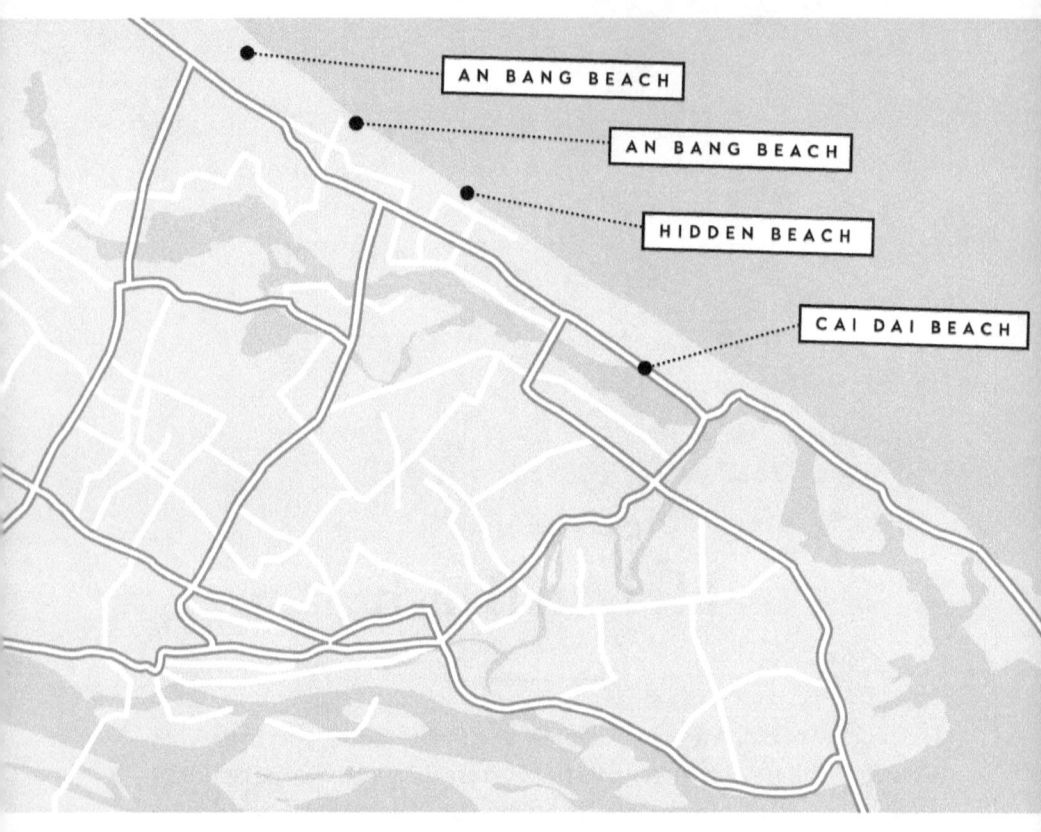

CHAPTER 9: HOI AN BEACH

Areas to Know in Hoi An Beach

AN BANG BEACH

This is where I prefer to stay as you'll find the most places to eat and some of the best accommodation! Here, the sands are dotted with colorful umbrellas and sun loungers, and the air is filled with the scent of sunscreen and the sound of laughter. The beachfront is lined with bustling restaurants and bars, making it an ideal spot for those seeking a day of fun and frolic.

HIDDEN BEACH

It really is hidden. From the main road in Hoi An, you take a right when you get to the coastal highway. About 5 minutes up the road, there is a tiny jungle road that leads to a small stretch of beach where you can enjoy more privacy than Cua Dai Beach and cozy beach bars. Look for Wild Beach Restaurant where you can spend the day snacking and drinking. Take your pick- both have lounge chairs and umbrellas for guests where you can sink your toes in the sand and soak up the sun. Some days the waves here are too intense to swim and others, they are perfect. Fingers crossed.

CUA DAI BEACH

People used to claim that Cua Dai beach is more serene and quiet than the other beaches, but the secret is out! Cua Dai is now the most popular stretch of beach and for good reason. Cua Dai Beach is the biggest and has plenty of restaurant options that provide lounge chairs and umbrellas with full beer and food service. It's consistently listed as one of the best beaches of Vietnam for its pristine white sand, turquoise water and gentle waves.

HA MY BEACH

Finally, there's the lesser-known Ha My Beach, a serene and pristine stretch of sand that is a dream for solitude seekers. If you've got a scooter, it's worth checking out. There are a few places to grab a beer or a smoothie. Or better yet, bring a picnic.

CHAPTER 9: HOI AN BEACH

Where to Stay in Hoi An Beach

AN BANG HIDEAWAY

You are literally steps from the beach down a little hidden beach path! You're so close that you can hear the waves from your outside patio! An Bang Beach Hideaway's location couldn't be better because it is on the very south side of the beach where the fishermen hang out. More fishermen, less tourists, in fact! It feels much more private than the rest of the beach. After a day of sunning, take a quick shower then walk the sandy path in the other direction and you'll hit my favorite An Bang Beach restaurants, Mr Hoà's Kitchen and An Bang Beach Village Restaurant. Ps. No shoes required for your whole stay here.

Budget: $$
Where: An Bang Beach   **Book Here:**

....

THE HAPPY BIRD B&B

The Happy Bird is a magical little oasis on the same sandy path as An Bang Beach Hideaway. This is a collection of traditional bungalows in a tropical garden run by the most lovely hosts who pour so much love and care into their guests' experience. As a digital nomad, I loved the cafe with comfortable spots to open my laptop and check my email while sipping on a latte or nourishing my body with smoothie bowls in their cafe, Yesh Tribe.

Budget: $$
Where: An Bang Beach   **Book Here:**

WANDERLUST

The most beautiful hostel in town is Wanderlust. There's a big bright pool surrounded by palm trees with boho vibes all around. Come with your schedule open because they offer free food tours on Fridays, free family dinner Wednesdays and other events that make it easy to connect with other travelers while connecting to Vietnamese culture. They have both dorms and private rooms, take your pick!

Budget: $
Where: An Bang Beach   **Book Here:**

UNDER THE COCONUT TREE

You've been dreaming of this place, I guarantee it. Little Vietnamese bamboo huts in a palm tree garden with glimmering lanterns! Welcome to your little Vietnam paradise! Rooms are simple but cozy, and if you prefer, there are dorms here too. You're just a two minute walk to the beach and every morning, breakfast is a little adventure as you're sent to a restaurant nearby with a breakfast voucher to go fill up on banana pancakes and coffee. This is the kind of place that you book for two nights and end up staying four. Just wait and see.

Budget: $
Where: 2-minute walk to An Bang Beach   **Book Here:**

THE SEASIDE BUNGALOW

Bonfire on the beach, anyone? This beachy homestay feels more like a summer camp for adults. The hosts do a great job of getting guests to gather for big family dinners or bonfires on the beach. And there is a restaurant and bar on site with a pool table that makes mingling easy. Best of all, The Seaside Bungalow is located just south of An Bang Beach on Ha My Beach, which isn't the most popular beach, but that just means less people besides the ones at your homestay! Yes the rooms are incredibly simple, but they are clean and have air conditioning. You don't need much more than that here.

Budget: $
Where: 3-minute walk from Ha My beach   **Book Here:**

VICTORIA HOI AN BEACH RESORT & SPA

If rustic isn't your thing and you're more of a beach resort type of traveler, I've got the place for you. Stay in an ocean-view room at Victoria and sleep with the windows open so that you can fall asleep to the sound of the ocean waves crashing on the shore. In the morning, head to the pool where you'll sip cocktails under the sun. Best of all, the beach is very private. You share it only with fishermen and a few locals - no tourists here (well, besides you, of course).

Budget: $$$
Where: Cua Dai Beachfront   **Book Here:**

CHAPTER 9: HOI AN BEACH

Where to Eat in Hoi An Beach

COSY CORNER

I could eat here every day. It's the spot where expats come regularly for breakfast and coffee and seem to know the staff on a personal basis. It's good vibes all around. Order the avocado toast that comes with bacon, feta and a poached egg. If you don't like poached eggs, do like me and ask for scrambled eggs on the side. Ps. The wifi is good. Come here to check your emails and get a little work done before a day at the beach.

⊙ **Open:** 7am-6pm
♥ **Where:** An Bang Beach

YESH TRIBE

My favorite place to stay is also my favorite place for a healthy brunch or breakfast. The Choco Locco smoothie bowls is a must, as is the Protein Bowl. You get sweet, fresh, and nutritious food for great prices! After eating so much rice and noodles, your body will begin to crave this stuff! They also offer an array of smoothies and kombucha! Heaven!

⊙ **Open:** Monday-Saturday, 7:30am - 3pm
♥ **Where:** An Bang Beach
♥ @YeshTribe

BUNGALOW BEACH BAR

It's not actually on the beach but they do have a pool! Eat here and you can get in that pool! No extra charge! They have burgers and draft beer. Come back on Fridays at 7:30 for live music. There's really not more to say other than the staff are friendly and the prices aren't too pricey. Check out their Facebook for events!

⊙ **Open:** 10am-midnight (opens at 4pm on Mondays)
♥ **Where:** An Bang Beach
❶ facebook.com/Bungalowbeachbar

SHORE CLUB

A trendy beach club bar without the beach club admission prices. Shore Club is a very photogenic spot with big blue and white beachclub-style beds under big umbrellas on an all-white deck overlooking the ocean. I ordered the shrimp spring rolls which were filling enough for lunch, but they also have noodle dishes and sandwiches, along with IPAs and cocktails! When you're done, head straight down onto the shore where you can rent a beachfront cabana, chair or bed for the day.

Open: 7:30am-9pm
Where: An Bang Beach
shoreclubvietnam.com

SIDENOTE ABOUT BEACH RESTAURANTS: There are dozens of Vietnamese beachfront seafood restaurants with tanks of fresh seafood that you would presume would be delicious...but I have only found terrible service, strange portions, messy kitchens and chain smoking staff at these places. I suppose you trade the view for the quality. For seafood, stick to my recommendations.

MR HOA'S KITCHEN AND RESTAURANT

Hidden down a colorful little alley by the beach, this may quickly become your go-to spot for dinner. Start with a mango mojito and samosas. Follow that with grilled red snapper with garlic & chili. Don't be surprised if you make friends here. I met a British couple here (and drank with them) and every night I walked by, they were sitting with a new couple, drinking. People come here to eat and talk and chat. It's just very friendly energy and delicious food! Pro Tip: When it's pouring down rain, come here for a wonderful atmosphere!

Open: 11am - 10pm
Where: An Bang

AN BANG VILLAGE RESTAURANT

One of the best dinners I've had in Vietnam, I only wish I had more dinners to keep coming back here so I could try everything on the menu. Order the banh xeo rolls, whole grilled snapper and the green papaya salad. Fresh, flavorful and a bargain! I also saw many people eating fresh scallops grilled on a little BBQ right in the alley and lots of shrimp and chicken on sticks! Eat here, take photos and tag me @sologirlstravelguide so I can be jealous.

Open: 11am - 10pm
Where: An Bang (right next to Mr Hoa's Kitchen and Restaurant)

CHANGOS

For after-dinner drinks, go to this other hidden alley spot! Changos has a backyard atmosphere with a pool table, chess and occasionally, live music. This is the kind of place where you're sure to meet strangers that become friends. Don't be afraid to come here alone! The barmen will make sure that you feel seen and are taken care of with a cocktail and great conversation.

🕓 **Open:** 6pm - midnight
📍 **Where:** Down a small alley off the main road (GoogleMaps has got you)

CHAPTER 9: HOI AN BEACH

Things to Do in Hoi An Beach

Here's my pro tip for planning activities in Hoi An.

When you're in the Ancient City, there is plenty to see and it's easy to get around. But when you're at the beach, obviously you're a bit far removed. So I recommend scheduling your tours that include free pick-up for when you're staying at the beach. Let them pick you up and drop you back off. No taxis needed! Here are three adventures not to miss...☞

MY SON SANCTUARY

In a valley surrounded by two mountain ranges and picturesque countryside, lies My son sanctuary. This place is a cluster of ruined Hindu temples dating back to as early as the 4th century and is a magnificent display of unique architecture that bears witness to an ancient civilization that is now extinct.

Here, you will find a complex of 70 edifices crafted from sandstone and reinforced with red bricks. Back in the day, this was a place of worship for the Cham people as well as a burial ground for their royalty. Now regarded as a Unesco World Heritage site, this little haven gives you a glimpse into a civilization long forgotten.

💰**Budget:** 100k VND

🕒**Open:** All day but best to visit early to avoid the hot afternoons

You can go DIY but I recommend this tour that picks up from Hoi An:

5AM TOUR FOR EARLY RISERS

I prefer to take this tour while I'm at the beach where there isn't much sightseeing. As this tour includes pick-ups, they'll pick you up early and drop you back at the beach just in time for sunbathing.

CHAM ISLAND

You will be recommended to go snorkeling at Cham Island, but what you will see is dead corals and crowded waters. The marine life is being inundated with travelers, gasoline and sunscreen. It's best not to participate.

CHAPTER 9: HOI AN BEACH

How to Get Around Hoi An Beach

WALK

Especially if you're staying in An Bang. You walk everywhere!

GRAB TAXI

Want to head to a beach bar further down the road? Just jump in a GrabTaxi.

BICYCLE

You can always bike around. You can even bike over to the Ancient City in about 30 minutes. Easy peasy.

✎ TRAVEL NOTES:

....

....

....

....

....

....

CHAPTER 9: HOI AN BEACH

How to Get to Hoi An Beach

OPTION ONE: FLY INTO DA NANG

Da Nang has an airport that connects to bigger airports in the region and Hoi An is just a 30-40 minute drive.

From the airport...

→ You can get a GrabTaxi

→ Or arrange a ride with a longtime local friend of mine. His name is Kieu Peck. He offers the cheapest price: 200k from Da Nang to Hoi An. Write him on Facebook here: facebook.com/hai.kieu.5264

OPTION 2: MAKE YOUR WAY TO DA NANG IN A BUS

From there, you can hire a taxi or organize a ride with your hotel to pick you up in Da Nang and to drive you 30 minutes along the coastal highway, passing beach resorts and secret beach roads that you wouldn't even know were there (until I tell you about them later). You'll then turn off the coastal road towards Hoi An where you'll pass long stretches of bright green rice paddies with water buffalo working the day away.

OPTION 3: GET DROPPED IN HOI AN

When you're coming from the north, you can get on a bus that drops you directly in Hoi An center (you'll still enjoy the scenery I mentioned above). Once in the center, it is very easy to just walk or get a ride to your hotel.

CHAPTER TEN

Da Nang

DAYS NEEDED:

1 night

BEST FOR:

Night markets and catching a flight from Da Nang Airport

CHAPTER TEN

Da Nang

Da Nang is the 3rd biggest city in Vietnam, home to tall skyscraper condos, a bustling middle-class population, a few universities, a decent sized expat + digital nomad community, and a pickleball court. Despite all of this, Da Nang is quite a sleepy little city with not too much to offer tourists outside of a couple viewpoints and night markets. YES night markets! Nowadays, I stop over in Da Nang just for one night so that I can hit up the wild night markets…and then if I'm still hungry, go get some shrimp on a stick at a local restaurant. Danang is worth a visit just to eat.

Da Nang is also home to long stretches of white sand beaches with resorts, condos, and tour agencies lining their perimeter, which is great if you want to be a digital nomad here. This is one of the most popular digital nomad cities in the world. If you want to slow down for a month, Da Nang might be worth getting to know. But odds are, you're just passing through and my honest advice would be to come here, eat, and then carry on.

CHAPTER 10: DA NANG

Areas to Know in Da Nang

BAC MY AN

This is the area I usually choose to stay. It's between the beach and the night markets, and is walking distance to some cool bigger markets.

HAI CHUA

Hai Chua is known as the commercial center of Da Nang. This is where urban activity happens, and you can find their main theater and shopping center here.

AN THUONG

Hai Chua may be where the market is, but An Thuong has all the best cafes. You'll have tons of variety, and it's a great place to ask around if you're still figuring out where to go.

BACH DANG

At night, Bach Dang just lights up, and not in a wild party way! The side of the city near the river gives off a really chill vibe with all its lights and cafes.

BEACHES TO KNOW

THANH BINH BEACH

The main strip of beach in Da Nang, you'll have instant access to Thanh Binh Beach when your bus pulls into town or when you drive in from the airport. It's decent for a day of sun tanning, but not extremely impressive in terms of beauty.

NON NUOC BEACH

20 minutes from Da Nang is the most beautiful beach in the area. With soft white sand with lots of people! It's a beautiful beach but just plan to share it with other beach lovers.

MY KHE BEACH

Once listed in Forbes Magazine as one of the 'World's Most Luxurious Beaches, My Khe Beach is now home to upscale resorts like the Hyatt and smaller boutique resorts.

Along this beach is where all the seafood restaurants are! If you're looking to hang around the beach or just eat good food, this is the place to go.

FUN FACT! Da Nang is one of Vietnam's most important port cities. It was founded in 1901 and it's the largest seaport in central Vietnam. It's a hub for the East-West Economic Corridor, linking commerce between Myanmar, Thailand, Laos and Vietnam.

CHAPTER 10: DA NANG

Where to Stay in Da Nang

DAISY BOUTIQUE HOTEL

When you want to be alone but not invisible - staying in a small boutique hotel is the way to go. No face goes unnoticed here, but you still have plenty of privacy. Daisy Boutique Hotel is ideal for first-timers in Da Nang who want to explore, swim and feel looked after by the enthusiastically sweet staff that love to share recommendations and tips! My pro tip for this hotel is to get a pool-access room! It's great for a quick morning dip and even better for people watching.

Budget: $$
Where: Bac My An

Book Here:

PAVILION HOTEL

Language barriers are no barrier at Pavilion, the staff speaks English! Looking for a place to stay that has the familiar amenities from back home and within walking distance of one of the most beautiful beaches in Asia? Look no further than Pavilion Hotel. This beachfront beauty is located directly along the My Khe Beach district and offers free use of bicycles, restaurant with complimentary breakfast, fitness center, hot tub, rooftop pool with views of the city and the ocean, and much more.

Budget: $$
Where: My Khe Beach district

Book Here:

MAI BOUTIQUE VILLA

I literally love this place because it's cheap, clean and is a 7-minute walk to the beach! It requires no thinking, planning or worrying. Just drop your bags, take a hot shower and go out for street food or to put your toes in the sand. The staff are always at your service, and they're a big help when it comes to information about the area. The on-site bar and restaurant serves some of the best Vietnamese food and drinks, too (also for cheap)/

Budget: $$
Where: Past the Song Han Bridge

Book Here:

FUN FACT! Da Nang is known for it's flavorful Central Vietnamese Cuisine. These are some of the most typical dishes you should try:

→ **Quảng, bún chả cá** *(fish ball noodle soup)*

→ **Bánh tráng cuốn thịt heo** *(dry pancake roll with pork)*

→ **Banh xeo** *(crispy pancake)*

→ **Nem lui** *(lemongrass pork skewers).*

Ps. This is a picture of balut. I dare you to google it).

And talking about food...

CHAPTER 10: DA NANG

Where to Eat in Da Nang

THE CHEAP CHICKEN SPOT

Officially called "Chân - Cánh Gà Nướng Hai Còi 08" - a friend of mine who has lived here in Danang for two years took me to this local spot where you order chicken on a stick! You sit in plastic stools and yell to the waiters when you want more chicken on a stick or cheap beer. And you can yell a lot because the food is so cheap! Crispy fried chicken wings are only .75 cents! The grilled pork belly and grilled shrimp are also a must!

◎ **Open:** 3pm - midnight
♥ **Where:** Bac My An

♥ **Google Maps:**

....

NIGHT MARKETS:
Chợ Đêm Sơn Trà Night Market

It's all about the night markets here. That's the only reason I come to Da Nang. They've got great night markets! Take a grab taxi to SH Beer Da Nang and you'll be dropped in

PRO TIP! Plan a local foodie evening like this…

→ Khu Ẩm thực đêm Helio for a beer and a snack.
→ Chợ Đêm Sơn Trà Night Market for a beer, some more snacks and shopping.
→ The Cheap Chicken Spot to fill up on chicken, shrimp and beer.

the best night market in town - full of food, trinkets to take home as souvenirs, spots to drink beer, music, massages, and world-class people watching. There are no directions or recommendations for this night market because a night market is all about the element of surprise and spontaneity! Let your eyes do the picking! Oh but I do recommend picking up some quiet and quirky keychains while you're here. You'll see what I mean....

Open: 6pm - midnight
Where: On the east side of the Dragon Bridge

Khu Ẩm thực đêm Helio

I recommend night market hopping. Helio night market is a bit more tame and modern than the other one. You'll find a big beer garden with an array of beers, live music and places to sit with your balut, ice cream or fresh seafood. Is this my #1 favorite night market? No. Is it worth a visit if you have time? Yes.

Open: 5:30pm - 10:30pm
Where: On the east side of the Dragon Bridge

PIZZA 4 P'S

Don't leave this country without trying Pizza 4 P's in one of the big cities in Vietnam! Any pizza that comes with a fresh ball of mozzarella on top, just to be rolled out at the table is worth an order! You haven't lived until you've tried it! Make a reservation online and request to sit at the bar so that you can watch the pizza being made!

Open: Daily 10am-10:30pm
Where: There are multiple locations, I recommend the Hoang Van Thu location.
Reserve a table either on Google or here: https://pizza4ps.com/

....

PHO 75

Looking for a local adventure? Staying loyal to the Southern way of making Pho, tender pieces of raw beef are placed in hot clear broth where they cook right before your eyes. The broth is very light, waiting for you to spice it up to your liking with chili sauce, soy, lime, and hot sauce. This street food stall is the OG of Pho in Da Nang.

Open: 8am-8pm (closed Thursday)
Where: 12 minute drive from Bac My An

CHAPTER 10: DA NANG

Things to Do in Da Nang

PLAY PICKLEBALL

(THAT'S MY BAREFOOT BOYFRIEND. HE DOESN'T KNOW THAT I PUBLISHED A PHOTO OF HIM...)

If you follow me on Instagram, you know that I am obsessed with Pickleball and tell everyone who will listen that traveling with your pickleball paddle is a great way to make friends! Well here in Danang there are two outdoor courts in the middle of a park! I forgot to pack sneakers so I played barefoot and the court was smooth enough that I didn't lose a toe.

To find it, type this on Google Maps: Công viên KDC Nhà Máy Cao Su (GoogleMaps "Pickleball Pin" is incorrect)

SCUBA DIVING

Right off the coast of Da Nang, you can find a colorful collection of coral and shoals of fish, as well as abundant marine life. Sign up for some fun dives or get your Open

Water Certification in Da Nang. Most of your dives will be done 18km off the coast near the Cham islands where the best underwater sites can be found.

Try Da Nang Scuba. They're reputable, fun and PADI certified.

Open Water Course Price: $260 / 6 million
Duration: 3 Days

GET A TATTOO AT LAMENT TATTOO

While in Hoi An, I was non-creepily admiring the artwork on my super-tattooed host's body. He told me that this is where he goes for his tattoos. If you're looking to get a tattoo in Vietnam, Danang is going to be the cleanest place to do it as this is certainly the cleanest city. Afterwards, take a few days to let it heal rather than going straight to the beach or getting sweaty outside.

Open: 9am-6pm
Where: Bac My An
www.facebook.com/lamenttattoo

CHAPTER 10: DA NANG

Sightseeing & Culture in Da Nang

DRAGON BRIDGE AT NIGHT

Photographers, get your camera ready. The Dragon Bridge over the Han River is designed to look like a fire-breathing dragon that lights up at night, reflecting off of the water below. Take a walk along the riverside, buy some snacks from vendors, and take some great Instagram-worthy shots of the 666-meter long beast. And every Wednesday at 9pm the dragon breathes fire! To get the ideal viewing spot, head to the Bach Dang Street area on the eastern bank of the Han River. There's a pedestrian walkway along the riverbank that provides an excellent vantage point to watch the fire-breathing performance.

♀Where: Phuoc Ninh
◔Best Times: Wednesday at 9pm - but get there around 8:30 pm

CHAPTER 10: DA NANG

Daytrips from Da Nang

HAI VAN PASS

You've read about this pass in the Hue section. Hai Van Pass is the mountain road that also straddles the coast line. You've got lush green jungle on one side and deep blue water on the other. The road is windy yet wide, making for a fun day of pure adventure on your way to Hue.

The whole trip takes about 3.5 hours and there are plenty of little snack bars and cafes along the way. If you want to get hyped up about this drive, it was featured on an episode of Top Gear and is every bit as amazing in real life as it is on screen.

Note that you can do this journey in 3 different sequences:

→ Hoi An to Hue
→ Da Nang to Hue
→ Or flip those two around and go the other direction

HOW TO GET AROUND DA NANG

WALK

You'll find more sidewalks in Da Nang than other parts of Vietnam. There is lots to see on foot and the area is generally pretty safe.

GRAB TAXI

Grab Bikes and taxis are everywhere! Grab Bikes costs around $1-$2 and Grab Cars typically cost $2-$3 depending where you're going. Install this app ASAP.

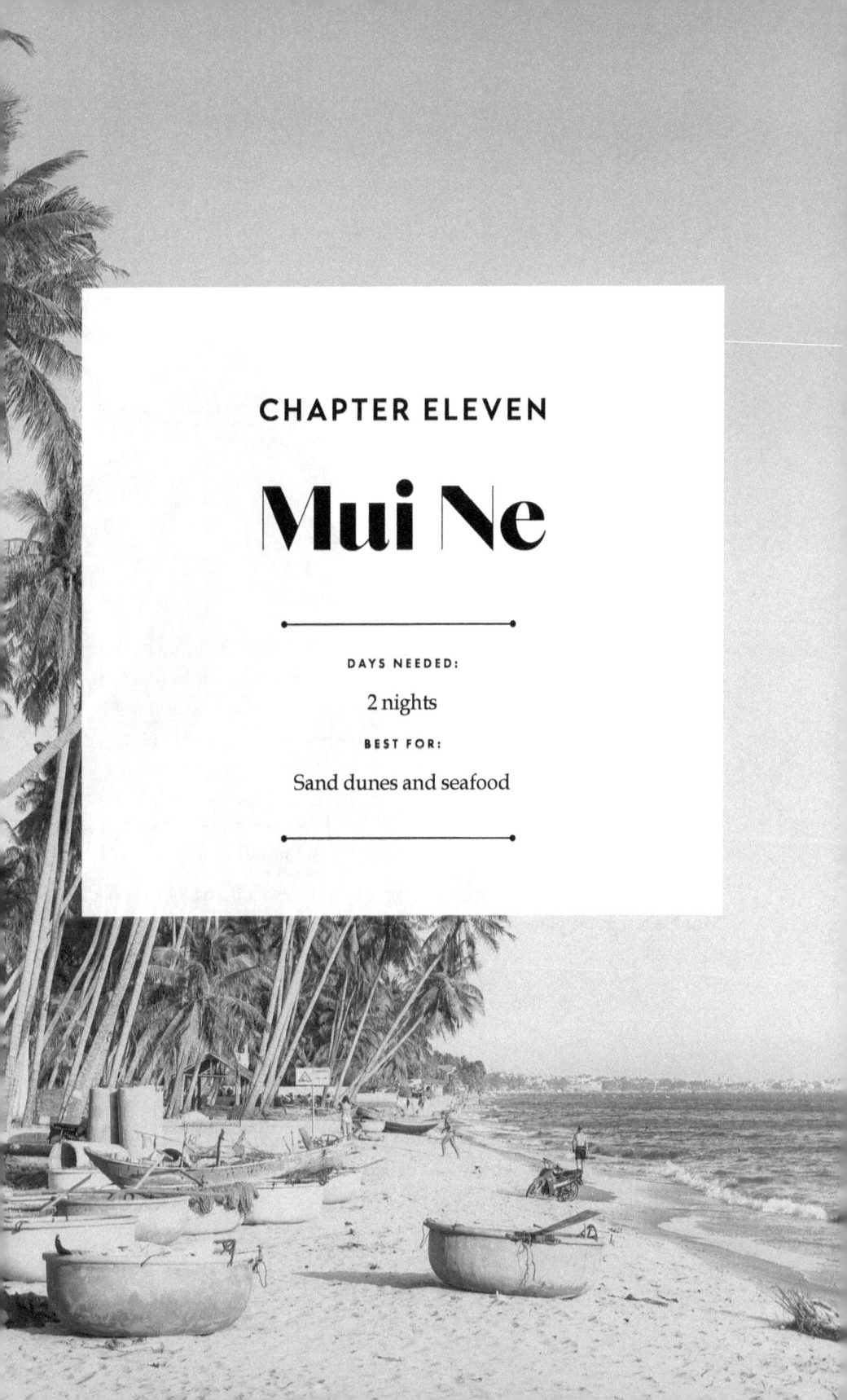

CHAPTER ELEVEN

Mui Ne

DAYS NEEDED:

2 nights

BEST FOR:

Sand dunes and seafood

CHAPTER ELEVEN

Mui Ne

Mui Ne used to be a sleepy fishing village, but it's blossomed into a bustling tourist hotspot over the years. The town's claim to fame? Its mind-blowing sand dunes. Seriously, these dunes will make you feel like you've stumbled into the Sahara. It's like a real-life desert in the middle of Vietnam!

Mui Ne is also renowned for its year-round warm weather and strong breezes, making this a great place for wind and kite surfers.

Whether you're seeking adventure, relaxation, or fresher than fresh seafood, Mui Ne is a good place to stop for a few days.

FUN FACT! The name of "Mui Ne" has different origins, but it's believed that it came from the fishermen in the past. Whenever a strom came, they would hide in a cape, which was called "Mui" in Vietnamese. And the word for hide was "Ne".

CHAPTER 11: MUI NE

Areas to Know in Mui Ne

MUI NE WARD

Mui Ne Ward is the fishing town of Binh Thuan. Though the entire area is generally called Mui Ne, it's actually the port area where all the fishing boats are. Marvel at the everyday activity of the local people and watch how they catch the country's most popular seafood.

PHAN THIET CITY

Resort City! The capital of the Binh Thuan Province is basically a 57.4-kilometers of coastline, beaches, and fishing areas! Water sports and seafood of all kinds is what attracts the tourists here. It's famous for all their international and Vietnamese bars and restaurants as well as their cheap hostels! Ho Chi Minh and Hanoi are also a short drive away. Enjoy dragon and seafood as you watch the waves.

HAM TIEN WARD

It's a little confusing, but what most people call Mui Ne is actually Ham Tien. It's actually the place between Mui Ne and Phan Thiet. This is where the massive kitesurfing craze began. The best time to go is from October to March, and the peak season is December to January. Aside from that, there's also tons of sailing, windsurfing, and kayaking rentals in this area.

PHU HAI WARD (Remainder of the Ancient Cham Culture)

On the hill just northeast of Phan Thiet is Phu Hai, and remnants of the ancient Cham culture can be found here. They were an ethnic group that had Austronesian origins (people who originated from Taiwan and subsequently spread across Southeast Asia, the Pacific, and Indian Oceans). You can also find the most amazing sand sculptures in the area.

CHAPTER 11: MUI NE

Where to Stay in Mui Ne

THE CLIFFS RESORT & RESIDENCE

It really doesn't get any more Kardashian than this. The Cliffs is one of those resorts that you see on TV, with Jacuzzis overlooking the water and sexy swimming pools meant for slow motion diving, but without the celebrity price tag. It's not a total guilt-free spend but at $165, it's a bucket list sleepover that every solo girl should experience once in her life. Live a little!

Budget: $$$
Where: 25-minute drive away from the White Sand Dunes

Book Here:

SUNSEA RESORT

Their world-class food and drinks are definitely one of the things guests love about this resort. International and Thai cuisine is the specialty in their restaurant Sukhothai. You can also enjoy a wide range of beer, wine, cocktails, and other beverages in their Beach bar. All the rooms are designed to your liking with TVs and DVDs. There's even hot tubs and Jacuzzis if you ask for it!

Budget: $$$
Where: Nguyen Dinh Chieu Street

Book Here:

LOTUS VILLAGE RESORT

Get a feel of traditional Vietnamese architecture with Lotus Village. It'll feel like you're in some exotic location rather than just the regular tropical hotel. Enjoy the sea breeze as you relax with their spa and massage treatments. You'll feel so at peace you'd never want to leave!

Budget: $$
Where: Phan Thiet City

Book Here:

iHOME BACKPACKER RESORT

Private beachfront access on a budget? Yes, please. This is backpacker paradise with a big pool overlooking the waves! Plan to be social when you come! They have a 1-hour free flow beer party every evening, movie nights, hammocks, a pool table and games galore! They have private rooms and dorm rooms. The dorms are so cheap they're practically free.

Budget: $
Where: Hoa Bin Street

Book Here:

EVA HUT HOSTEL

Boho and contemporary all at the same time, this boutique homestay is like you've stepped into one of your Pinterest boards. The attention to detail in decor matches the attention to detail in the service and hospitality. Have a seat at the bar and chat with the bartenders as they make you a margarita to take straight onto the beach. Yes, this hostel is beachfront, too! There are big beds for lounging and hammocks under palm trees where you can read a book or take a nap. They have dorm rooms but if you can swing it, I recommend the studio with seaview.

Budget: $
Where: Beachfront, East Ham Tien

Book Here:

CHAPTER 11: MUI NE

Where to Stay in Mui Ne

DONG VUI FOOD COURT

Crowded and fun is what the name says, and it's definitely true when you get there. This food park has practically every cuisine you're hoping to try, and some of the best restaurants in the area can be found here too. Local, international, vegan, and more! You'll have to come back a second time if you want to try all their stalls.

NOTE: Opening hours vary per season. Individual stalls also have their own opening hours so if you're looking for one store in particular, better check in advance.

Open: Daily 7:30am - 11pm
Where: Nguyen Dinh Chieu Street

SURFING BIRD'S WOK

Your Asian experience isn't complete without noodles and here in Mui Ne, this is the place to go. They specialize in Asian and Chinese dishes all cooked on the wok. Fried noodles with mushroom and black pepper beef are a must-try! They also have great homemade lemonade and cheesecake. It's the equivalent of Asian soul food all under one roof.

Open: Daily 12pm - 10:30pm
Where: Dong Vui Food Court
Address: 246/2B Nguyen Dinh Chieu, Mui Ne, Phan Thiet

EL CAFE VEGETARIAN FOOD

You think finding good vegan food is hard in Vietnam? Well, the owner of this restaurant thought so, too! Try a wide range of international cuisine made vegan and vegetarian. Their food is moderately priced and packed with spices that you've probably never heard of. Take note of their vegan cheese and sauce as it was made by the owner himself!

Open: Daily 9am - 11pm
Where: Dong Vui Food Court
Address: 246/2B, Nguyen Dinh Chieu, Mui Ne, Phan Thiet

CHAPTER 11: MUI NE

Fun Things to Do in Mui Ne

VISIT MUI NE FISHING VILLAGE

If you want to experience local life, Mui Ne Fishing Village should be included in your holiday. This small village has a very impressive coastline that is colored with fishing boats of all shapes and sizes. There are food carts and restaurants along the coast, serving Vietnamese signatures at an affordable price. You can order fresh seafood from a vendor and they'll cook it up on the spot.

◉ **Best time to go:** If you want to visit without battling the huge tours visiting the village or walking under the scorching sun, it is best to visit in the early morning or in the afternoon.

THE WHITE SAND DUNES

When you arrive at this place, you may find yourself asking "Did I just teleport to the Sahara?" The White Sand Dunes are about 35 minutes north of Mui Ne and covers a vast expanse of land that stretches as far as you can see. Locals call these dunes the Bau Trang or "the White Lake". In the monsoon season, they say the winds change the location of the sandhills scattered in the dunes, making for fresh adventures.

Sign up for a tour and pile into a big ass jeep that can handle the rolling roads. When you get there, you'll hop on an ATV to zoom around or grab a sand surfing board and shred.

☆ **Best tour:** Go with your hostel or book this tour…

WALK THE FAIRY STREAM

Peaceful and adventurous, this little stream is nothing more than a small ankle-to-knee deep river that travels through forests, sand dunes and rock formations- but is beyond enjoyable. The 'fairy' name comes from the blue, red, white, and green sands mixing in with the stream, creating a whimsical piece of heaven. Kick your shoes off and enjoy the cool, clean water rushing over your skin.

PRO TIP! The tour to the White Sand Dunes usually includes a detour to the stream. You can get this as a package deal.

SLIDE ON THE RED SAND DUNES

Right down the road from Sand Dunes Beach Resort near central Mui Ne lies a big rolling hill of red sand. When you drive by, there will be Vietnamese kids on the side of the road, waving you down to give you plastic slides where you can sled down the sand dune. It's a fun little detour before or after the beach.

PRO TIP! Don't leave your bags with these kids. They're sneaky.

♥ Where: Mui Ne Town

CHAPTER 11: MUI NE

Markets & Shopping in Mui Ne

Oyster heaven, Mui Ne is full of pearl shops everywhere you turn. You can get glossy white pearls and rare black pearls of every quality in this city, usually in pearl boutique shops that all seem to sell around the same price.

And if you're not in the market for pearls, head to a local market for some of the best shopping around.

HAM TIEN MARKET

As far as markets are concerned, Ham Tien's is relatively small, but the goods there are just as diverse. Around 6 to 9 in the morning is their busiest because everyone is buying stuff for their own homes. Native food and packaged desserts are plenty here! Make sure to get some mangosteen and custard apples while you're at it.

⊙ **Open:** 5:30 am - 9pm
🏛 **Address:** Nguyen Dinh Chieu Street, Phan Thiet

PHAN THIET CENTRAL MARKET

With hundreds of markets, this market is the largest of its kind in Mui Ne and holds a ton of handicrafts. Paintings, bags, scarves, and ceramics made in ancient Cham styles can also be found here. There aren't a lot of places where you'll see Cham anything, so this is definitely a treat worth going for. Make sure you bring enough money!

⊙ **Open:** 5am - 6pm
🏛 **Address:** Intersection between Ly Thuong Kiet and Nguyen Hue Streets,

CHAPTER 11: MUI NE

How to Get Around Mui Ne

WALK

There's not much to see via walking, but you can easily reach some restaurants and beach bars if your hotel is on the main strip.

LOCAL BUS

To go into Phan Thiet Town, hop on a cheap bus. Blue Bus (#1) and Red Bus (#9) go from Mui Ne to Phan Thiet city center every 15-20 minutes. No bus stops; just go on to the closest main street in front of your resort or hostel and wave your hand when one passes by. Tickets are around 20k ($1).

MOTORBIKE TAXI

Motorbike Taxis hustle up and down the tourist area offering rides to the train station, bus station, restaurants, etc. Expect to pay $1-4 per ride.

RENT A SCOOTER

Instead of signing up for tours to the sand dunes or the beach, rent your own motorbike and drive along the chilled out coastal road to create your own tour!

IMPORTANT NOTE...

The traffic police in Mui Ne are constantly pulling western tourists over to check for a Vietnamese or International Driver's License. If you don't have ID to show, you might be shaken down for as much as $50. On that note, don't travel with any illegal greens on your person!

CHAPTER TWELVE

Dalat

DAYS NEEDED:

3 nights

BEST FOR:

Coffee, pho and cooler temperatures

CHAPTER TWELVE

Dalat

• — •

The first time I visited Dalat, I was startled to see that my coconut oil had hardened for the first time in months! That is because of Dalat's mountainous altitude where temperatures rarely exceed 30°C (86°F), earning Dalat the nickname "City of Eternal Spring". This makes Dalat the perfect place to put on a sweater, drink some hot coffee and warm up with a big bowl of Pho.

Snuggled into Vietnam's Central Highlands, Dalat is surrounded by beautiful pine forests, lakes and rolling hills and famous for its day trips to waterfalls, palaces and monasteries! Get ready for a different flavor of Vietnam…

FUN FACT! Da Lat is also called 'Le Petit Paris' because it has a mini-replica Eiffel Tower in the centre, and because it was a holiday destination for the French during French colonial times.

CHAPTER 12: DALAT

Areas to Explore in Dalat

Dalat is broken down into Wards (or "Phuongs" in Vietnamese) and unlike most cities the wards do not have names and are simply known as Ward 1, Ward 2, Ward 3, etc. The system is relatively simple to understand, with Ward 1 being the most central and then the numbers going up as you get further away from the city center. For frame of reference Bui Thi Xuan is fairly centrally located within Ward 1 and all of the guest houses and restaurants mentioned in this guide have the Ward number attached so you can see where they are in relation to the city center.

Dalat city center is pretty small, so most of the Wards are within easy walking distance of each other.

BUI THI XUAN STREET

Bui Thi Xuan (Ward 1) is ground zero for travelers in Dalat, dripping with reasonably priced local restaurants, bars and coffee houses. It's also the link to the maze of hostel streets and fun little souvenir shops. Bui Thi Xuan's central location within Dalat makes it a great base for those looking to spend a few days exploring the town without having to bus or cab around the city. It is also a great spot to organize those famous adventure tours that lure you up here, with multiple tour shops lining the street ready to take you to far flung corners of the countryside.

XUAN HUONG LAKE

This large man-made lake is just a short walk from Bui Thi Xuan Street. The lake is surrounded by beautiful flower gardens, a large golf course and Dalat's famous Palace Hotel. It's a great place to wander, smell the flowers and enjoy the region's cooler, spring-like climate with a cup of coffee in hand.

TUYEN LAM LAKE

This large lake is a fifteen-minute walk downhill from Truc Lam Pagoda and offers peace and relaxation, plus boats for hire and quaint local restaurants. There's often a local man offering to show you his classic car collection at the bottom of the walk (basically a Cadillac and an old Vespa rickshaw) but he's very sweet and is keen to practice his English. His cars are normally parked up outside one of the lake's restaurants for your viewing pleasure.

FUN VIETNAM FACT!

Lizard Fishing is one of Vietnam's most widespread hobbies. Ask a local and maybe they'll take you.

CHAPTER 12: DALAT

Where to Stay in Dalat

Listen. Dalat is not fancy. It's not new. It's not modern. Your hostels will be simple, and your bathrooms will be basic…but what these hostels and hotels lack in fancy amenities, they more than make up for in hospitality.

For a truly local homestay, don't be afraid to wander on your own in the back alleys to find a tiny family guest- so small that they don't advertise on the internet.

PRO TIP! In the summer, Vietnam's honeymooning couples come to town, so it pays to book ahead during this high season.

THE LAKE HOUSE

Wake up on the lake. Yes…ON. Cozy rooms with big windows that offer unobstructed views of the water and rolling hills are the epitome of travel goals. This cozy, peaceful guesthouse is located on Tuyen Lam Lake and offers up a far more secluded side of Dalat – while not being too far from the city center. You're just a short walk from monasteries, waterfalls and lakes- allowing you to take advantage of life off the beaten path. When you're in the mood for night markets and shopping, just hop in a free shuttle to town.

🏷️ **Budget: $$**   🌐 **Book Here:**

DALAT BACKPACKER'S ALLEY HOSTEL

There's a reason that Dalat Backpacker's Alley Hostel is often booked up... because they're the best in terms of hospitality and friendship. No, this isn't the Ritz. The dorms are pretty simple, and the bathrooms are outdated, but the hospitality is pristine. Anything you need from booking a bus to finding cough medicine – you'll get personal attention that is invaluable. Once you get to Ho Chi Minh City and start planning your trip up to Dalat, get online and book a bed. You'll be glad you did.

Budget: $ **Book Here:**

MOOKA'S HOME

When Dalat Backpacker Hostel is booked up, the next best thing (or maybe even the better thing - depending on what you're looking for) is Mooka's. When you check in, the staff give you a list of adventures and landmarks to help you visualize your stay. The dorm rooms are modern with comfy beds, a locker for your valuables and a curtain for privacy. The highlight of staying here however is the group BBQ dinner on the roof which makes it easy to meet people!

Budget: $ **Book Here:**

CHAPPI MOUNTAINS BUNGALOWS

If you want a really special experience in a cabin under the stars in the highlands off the beaten path, you need to book this airbnb for a night or two. This is the place of solitude, reflection and you-time. This is your chance to go outside your comfort zone, get on a local bus (which the hosts will help you organize) and do something different. You'll be glad you did.

Budget: $$

Look up "Chappi Mountains Bungalows" on Airbnb or Book here:

CHAPTER 12: DALAT

Where to Eat in Dalat

COFFEE HOUSES IN DALAT

No trip to Dalat would be complete without a buzz from the region's locally grown coffee. Dalat is so dense in coffee shops that you can barely move without falling into one.

LA VIET

They plant, process, roast and brew their own coffee! If you want to buy coffee to take home, this is the place to come! Be warned, however, you'll need a scooter to get here. But once here, you'll want to stay a few hours. Their coffee shop is stunning, modern and relaxed.

🕒 **Open:** 7am-10pm
📍 **This is the location you want:** 200 Nguyễn Công Trứ, Phường 8
facebook.com/coffeelaviet

BICYCLE UP CAFE

I'm about to make a controversial statement...Bicycle Up Cafe might be even better than La Viet in terms of atmosphere. It's cozier, the decor is whimsical, baristas have this cheerful Disneyland vibe to them and damn, that coffee is good. Not to mention, the food here is always on point! Plus, you don't have to haul your ass all the way over to the other side of town and back just to get your caffeine fix.

🕒 **Open:** 7am-10:30pm
facebook.com/Bicycleup

NOW COFFEE

If not now, then when? Visit this cute coffee shop with an outdoor garden to start your day the right way. Be sure to try their signature Vietnamese iced coffee, known as "cà phê sữa đá," for a true taste of local coffee culture. Pair your drink with a scrumptious selection of pastries, like their flaky croissants or chocolate cake!

Open: 7am-9:30pm
facebook.com/NOWBISTRO

ME LINH COFFEE GARDEN

You've never seen a coffee shop with a view like this before; I guarantee it. Me Linh Coffee Garden sits overlooking the area's bright green coffee farms, rolling hills, and reservoir- showing off where these pretty little beans come from. This coffee shop is fast becoming a mandatory stop on Dalat's tourist trail, so get here early to grab a table with a full view.

Open: 7am-6:30pm
facebook.com/melinhcoffeegarden

BRUNCH, LUNCH & DINNER

ONE MORE CAFE

Ignore the slightly odd decor (it's like going for tea at your nan's house) and jump into the amazing breakfasts at One More Cafe. The chefs here know how to whip up a smashed avocado on toast & a healthy Chia seed parfait just like you'd expect at a fancy schmancy brunch spot. The place is always full (a great sign) and you get to sit and eat your breakfast in a cozy armchair. The whole experience is quirky (unintentionally, I think) and delicious. How can you pass this up?

Open: 8am-9pm
facebook.com/onemorecafe77

GOC HA THANH

Goc Ha Thanh is the place to go to experience a Vietnamese obsession: hotpot. Here, you can dine on flavorful hotpots (they are one of the few places to offer a vegetarian hotpot), great curries and heaping plates of noodles! This place is so popular that it's always full. Located close to Dalat's night market, try to get there in the early evening.

Open: 12pm-8pm

CA RI VIT

There's no method to the madness here. This local spot cooks what they want, when they want. Sometimes it's pork, sometimes chicken, but most often than not, it's a duck and noodle dish that will change your life (Vegetarians and Vegans need not apply). You might have no idea what's being served up but get in line either way and prepare for a culinary adventure. Locals literally cue round the block just to get a bowl.

🕒 **Open:** Whenever they want (cause Vietnam) - If it's open you'll see the line of people waiting

PHO PHO EVERYWHERE!

With such a chilly mountain climate, you can find a pho spot on every street corner to warm your soul. Pull up a metal or plastic chair, use the good old 'point and order' tactic and wait for a massive bowl to be brought over. Garnish with lime, chili, and soy sauce and enjoy. Warning: these mom & pop bowls of pho tend to be ridiculously big and ridiculously cheap.

FUN PHO FACT! Pho, pronounced "fuh", is one of Vietnam's most iconic dishes. But even though it's so embedded in Vietnamese culture, it originated during the French colonial period, from the French classic beef stew "pot-au-feu". The Vietnamese adapted this soup into their own culture and ingredients and eventually Pho became a staple of Vietnamese cuisine.

CHAPTER 12: DALAT

Nightlife in Dalat

Nightlife in Dalat doesn't carry on much past midnight. But have no fear, hostels in the area pick up the slack. So, start drinking early with happy hours and sunset views at some of the best bars in town…

B21 BEER

B21 Beer is a large and busy bar with a 2-for-1 happy hour every day of the week, except for Saturdays. This is one of the bigger bars in Dalat and always has something to offer, whether it be live sports, live music or DJs- it's nice to just sit back and melt into the atmosphere. The bar caters mainly to westerners, and a traveler crowd. It's no surprise then that B21 Beer tends to get pretty lively most nights. Throw yourself in the new mix and you'll surely meet some new people and make some new friends.

☉ **Open:** 3pm-1am

100 ROOFS CAFE

If hobbits wanted a beer this is where they'd hang out. This place is part bar / part art installation and the weirdest beer experience you'll ever have. Happy hour is cheap, and the bar has multiple nooks and crannies to hide yourself away from the chilly night air while also providing the perfect place for a Tinder date (even in the mountains). While you're here, be sure to check out the surreal rooftop garden!

☉ **Open:** 8:30am-12am

··

STREET BEERS

One of the most common ways to enjoy the nightlife in Dalat is to buy a beer from a street vendor and just have a wander. Walk through the markets, people watch in the park, or snack as you go. Consider it a nightlife walking tour…

CHAPTER 12: DALAT

Sightseeing & Adventures in Dalat

ROYAL PALACES

Check out the collection of 3 royal palaces, formerly home to Emperor Bao Dai. Don't expect glitz and glamor, these palaces have seen better days and are in need of some TLC – but in terms of architecture and history, they are pretty cool and provide a glimpse into Vietnam's opulent imperial past.

💰 **Budget:** $1 USD/ 22k VND
🕐 **Open:** 7am-4pm (closed from 11 am-1:30 pm for lunch)

TRUC LAM PAGODA

This is your chance to visit an authentic working monastery. Wander through the beautiful gardens to the sound of windchimes and monks chanting; you are even able to join in on meditation classes. The pagoda's hilltop location offers staggering views of the surrounding area!

📍 **How to get there:** The best and most scenic way to reach Truc Lam Pagoda is by taking the cable car, taking you over coffee farms and local villages as you ascend. You can catch the cable car at Robin Hill (Thung Lung Tinh Yeu), which is located around 5 kilometers from the city center. Take a taxi to get there. The cable car ride takes you directly to the pagoda complex on Phung Hoang Mountain and usually costs around 100,000 to 200,000 VND (approximately $4 to $8) per person for a round trip.

💰 **Budget:** At the time of my last update, the entrance fee to Truc Lam Pagoda was around 30,000 VND (approximately $1.5) per person. This fee grants you access to the pagoda and its surroundings.

HANG NGA CRAZY HOUSE

Home to one of Vietnam's most avant-garde architects, this ever-evolving wonderland has been growing and manifesting for many years as the designer's dreams are brought to life in front of your eyes. The house is surreal and utterly outrageous- much like a scene out of Alice in Wonderland. You can wander around the house as you wish, easily spending a good few hours exploring its never ending corners.

BONUS! Hang Nga Crazy House also doubles as a mind-blowing hotel, with future plans to build a restaurant and under the sea nightclub here, too.

Budget: $2 USD / 45k VND
Open: 8:30am-7pm

GO CANYONING & RAPPELLING

The main attraction in Dalat is canyoning and rappelling! Hike up a rocky mountain, repel down a waterfall, swim in cool pools of fresh mountain water and slide down natural rock water slides. You'll set off on a group tour (expect others from your hostel to have come to Dalat for this exact tour) and have a wet and wild day full of adrenaline. You'll get tons of badass photos, as well, all of which will scare the shit out of your mom. You can do these tours with your hostel or hotel.

PRO TIP! If you're staying at a private hotel but want to meet some younger-aged people on your Canyoning adventure, walk into Dalat Backpackers to join their tour.

Otherwise, join this tour which is still social for a wider range of ages!

Budget: About $50 USD (and worth every penny)

ROLLER BLADE IN THE PARK AT NIGHT

Taking it back to the 90's, ya'll. When you're in Dalat, check out Dalat City Centre at night. There's a cement park full of teenagers and young 20-somethings roller skating along and doing tricks. They'll ride up alongside you and ask if you'd like to try for a small fee (you can always haggle this price).

♀Where: Near the Night Market

EASY RIDER TOURS

Also, not to be missed are Dalat's famous Easy Rider tours (but watch out, there are plenty of imitators that claim to be "Easy Riders" – everyone wants to be like the best). These tours involve hopping on the back of a motorbike and being whisked through Dalat's scenic and beautiful countryside.

There are plenty of routes that you can take that vary with waterfalls, mountains, distance, etc. Check 'em out at the shop and agree the price upfront. Once you are ready, hop on and prepare for what may well be the most enjoyable day of your trip!

Check them out here:

CHAPTER 12: DALAT

Shopping in Dalat

You'll find tons of little souvenir shops in Dalat alongside plenty of shops selling coffee of all kinds. But if you want the big-ticket items, check out Dalat's markets...

DAY MARKET

Ever wanted to up your swag game with some Abidas or Lewis Vuitton? No, those aren't typos...these are the awesome imitation brands that you can find at Dalat's Day Market. If you can put it on your body, you can buy it at this local friendly market and much more! Haggle hard; but with a smile.

NIGHT MARKET

Come evening time, Dalat's evening traders swap places with Dalat's day traders as Dalat's Day Market turns into Dalat's Night Market. Mainly concentrating on street food and entertainment, the streets around the crowded market become abuzz with locals and travelers alike. Lights, sounds, toys, and treasures- grab a walking beer and explore.

HOW TO GET AROUND DALAT

WALK

Dalat is small and mountainous. You can walk just about everywhere!

MOTORBIKE TAXI

There will be a man on just about every corner saying, "Hey, mo-to-bike". These guys are pretty cheap and can take you just about anywhere in the city.

RENT A SCOOTER

Dalat is pretty spread out, so if you want to cover a lot of ground, rent a motorbike for your visit. The roads are relatively wide, and the traffic isn't too chaotic- especially once you get out of the city center. The coastal roads are quite peaceful.

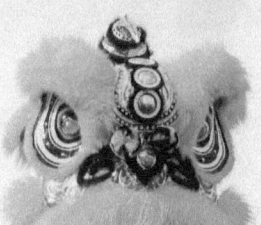

CHAPTER THIRTEEN

Ho Chi Minh City

(SAIGON)

DAYS NEEDED:

3-5 nights

BEST FOR:

History, street food and a little partying

CHAPTER THIRTEEN

Ho Chi Minh City

If there was ever a tale of two cities, Ho Chi Minh fits the bill. It's traditional and modern. Hectic and organized. Tied to the past and reaching for the future.

Formerly known as Saigon, this city has seen more than its fair share of dramatic history. In the late 1800s, Saigon was the center of the French trade in Indochina. The French colonial influence can still be seen today in its architecture, such as the iconic Central Post Office and Notre-Dame Cathedral. This period of French occupation left a lasting impact on the city's culture and cuisine, blending Vietnamese traditions with French influences.

By the 1950s, Saigon had become the capital of independent South Vietnam with dreams of embracing capitalism and countering the communist North. It was during this time that Saigon became heavily involved with American forces and served as the base for American military operations. The Vietnam War brought significant changes and challenges to the city.

In the end, the fall of Saigon to the communist North in 1975 marked a turning point in history. It brought an end to twenty years of war and resulted in an official name change of the city from Saigon to Ho Chi Minh City, in honor of the leader of the North.

Today, Ho Chi Minh City is still lovingly referred to as Saigon by locals and expats alike. Eight million people (and three million motorbikes) call this bustling place home.

From budget deals on accommodation to upscale rooftop bars, there's an adventure here for everyone. Immerse yourself in the city's center, enjoying the backpacker nightlife of Bui Vien. Venture out into China Town, Little Japan, and Little Korea to take advantage of the close cuisine proximity. Soak up some history and perspective at the War Remnants Museum, where you can see firsthand the impact of the Vietnam War through its powerful exhibits.

Ho Chi Minh City captures the essence of Vietnam's past, present, and future. Its blend of traditions and modernity, chaotic yet organized streets, and it's warm and resilient people make it a captivating destination for travelers. Whether you explore its historical sites, embrace the local culture, or simply immerse yourself in the vibrant atmosphere, Ho Chi Minh City promises an unforgettable experience that will leave a lasting impression for years to come.

Whatever you do, just make sure to leave with a bowl of Pho in your stomach and a coconut coffee in your hand. The rest will stick with you for years to come.

THE ROMAN CATHOLIC TAN DINH CHURCH

CHAPTER 13: HO CHI MINH CITY

Areas to Explore in Ho Chi Minh City

Unlike other cities in Southeast Asia, Ho Chi Minh is broken up into manageable, bite-sized pieces. Each of its twenty-four districts has a unique vibe and stands out among the crowd. Some are known for their nightlife and others for the best food in the city.

Let's highlight the most popular districts in Saigon, shall we?

DISTRICT 1

If you're a backpacker, odds are that you'll be staying in District 1. It's Ho Chi Minh's hotspot for hostels, bars, and restaurants. This is the epitome of backpacker life + close proximity to tours and sightseeing.

Start your day off with the district's many museums and architectural landmarks. There are parks, monuments, and the must-see War Remnants Museum within walking distance.

Afterwards, treat yourself to cheap food sold by street vendors on every corner. Next, plan to shop til you drop with markets galore selling knock-off handbags and handmade trinkets. Be prepared to haggle to your heart's desire.

When night hits, things get crazy around here! Locals and backpackers hit the streets for street food, bars, club hopping, or just sitting in plastic chairs with a beer and the best people watching you could ever imagine.

DISTRICT 2

As Vietnam's largest city, Ho Chi Minh attracts endless expats. The vast majority of these foreigners choose to live in District 2, giving it a uniquely Western feel in a city that is undoubtedly Asian. For a taste of what living abroad may look like (and for some of the comforts of home) checking out District 2 is a great idea for an afternoon adventure.

It's best to come here with an empty stomach, a cute outfit, and your camera ready for some Instagram action. You'll be spending the next few hours diving in and out of small hipster cafés and shops. With a little wander about, you'll find that street murals are aplenty. Leaving without a few selfies is a cardinal sin!

While you're here, check out Saigon Outcast, a popular bar that manages to mix beach energy with urban life. Aside from the great drinks, the graffiti-covered walls and industrial decor make for one of the coolest spots around.

DISTRICT 3

Get local in District 3. With fewer tourists and tourist attractions, you get the chance to mix in with resident Vietnamese who are simply going about their daily routines amongst beautiful French-style architecture and Buddhist traditions. In fact, District 3 is home to the vast majority of the city's Buddhist pagodas.

And for any foodies reading, District 3 is definitely the place to be in terms of local food! While Bahn Mi and Pho are delicious, you'll have ample opportunity to taste Vietnamese delicacies and dishes that are not so well known in the west.

☆ **You Can't Miss:** Women's Museum, Ky Dong Church, Archbishop's Palace, Xai Lot Pagoda, Vinh Nghiem Pagoda, and the Jade Emperor Pagoda

☆ **Where to Eat:** Nguyen Thien Thuat Street, Ky Dong Street, Vuon Chuoi Market, and the Phu Nhuan District.

PRO TIP! If you plan to visit Buddhist pagodas in District 3, dress for the occasion with an outfit that covers your knees and shoulders.

DISTRICT 5 (CHO LON)

I know, I know. If you wanted to experience China, you'd probably be there instead of Vietnam. However, you're so close to China that this is the next best thing! Why not experience the Chinese-Vietnamese fusion known as Cho Lon. This district boasts the largest market in all of Vietnam, Chinese temples...and of course, Chinese food.

Cho Lon literally translates to "big market". You'll understand why the simple name is so fitting after a visit to Binh Tay. It's a great spot to spend a few hours, eating your way through a variety of dishes and shopping for little trinkets to take home.

What makes District 5 so unique — despite every city in the world having a China Town — is its specific history. Throughout the 1970s, the government launched anti-Chinese campaigns in Ho Chi Minh City. They sought to remove the Chinese influence on Vietnam, and in turn worked to dismantle ChinaTown. Luckily, those efforts simply resulted in a neighborhood that is a unique mix of the two cultures, showing the resiliency of the people who live there.

☆ **You Can't Miss:** Binh Tay Market, Nghia An Hoi Quan Pagoda, Tam Son Hoi Quan Pagoda, and Thien Hau Pagoda.

DISTRICT 7 (PHU MY HUNG)

Sick of the smog, traffic, and crowds? District 7 may be the oasis you've been searching for! While still providing access to everything you love about Ho Chi Minh City, this district feels world's away from the city center and is worth a visit just for a few breaths of fresh air!

District 7 is Ho Chi Minh's second most popular expat neighborhood with all the modern amenities – resulting in a very diverse community. Here you'll find Little Japan and Little Korea nestled amongst countless western spots.

☆ **You Can't Miss:** Little Japan and Little Korea! Even if you're looking to stick to the city center's backpacker prices and vibes, it's interesting to see the stark contrast between the alleys of downtown and the broad, pristine streets of District 7. It's a picture-perfect example of the duality Ho Chi Minh City is known for.

CHAPTER 13: HO CHI MINH CITY

Best Tours in Ho Chi Minh City

Before we even get into where to stay and what to do, I must tell you that the best way to explore a city as complex as HCMC is with tour guides that show you layers of the city you might not discover on your own. Seriously, HCMC takes years to even scratch the surface so don't be a hero. Plan some tours! You can explore on your own and with this book in between.

FOOD TOURS

 Food and Culture with an All-Girl Team of Drivers

Affordable Big Group Tour

 Walking Street Food Tour with Local Students

Vegetarian Food Tour on Scooter

 Cooking Class and Wet Market Tour

Farm To Table Cooking Class

CULTURE & HISTORY TOURS

Hop-On Hop-Off Bus (yes, it's touristy but it's great and a dollar-saver)

 Mekong Delta and Chu Chi Tunnel Tour

Mekong Adventures - Boat, Bike and Kayak

 City Tours with Saigon Kiss Girls

Super Affordable City Tour

 Floating Market and Countryside

Best Chu Chi Tunnel

 2 Day Mekong And Market

Saigon on Cyclo

 Highlights And Gems

CHAPTER 13: HO CHI MINH CITY

Where to Stay in Ho Chi Minh City

PRO TIP! Splurge for a hotel that offers free airport pick up and now it's a save, not a splurge.

Ps. Accommodation prices fluctuate depending on the season. Throughout this book, you can take these prices as an average to get an idea if they fit your budget!

HOTEL DES ARTS SAIGON

Damn, this place is sexy and snuggly with a date-night-approved rooftop bar with an amazing cocktail menu, and the highest rooftop infinity pool in the city This is one of the most lavish hotels in Saigon while still being way cheaper than any other luxury hotel you'd find back home. Not to mention, the location is perfect for evening adventures and the staff go out of their way to make your visit as comfortable as possible.

Budget: $$$
Where: District 3

🌐 Book Here:

LA SIESTA SAIGON

Luxury seekers and spa lovers, this one's for you. This hotel offers easy access to the city's attractions while providing a luxurious retreat with its spa facilities and outdoor pool. After a refreshing dip, treat yourself to a gourmet meal at the on-site restaurant - the Cha Ca, a turmeric fish with dill, is a must-try. With spacious rooms and top-notch service, this hotel ensures a restful stay after a day of city exploration. Plus, the Independence Palace, a historic landmark, is just a short stroll away, adding a touch of history to your luxury stay.

Budget: $$$ **Where:** District 1

🌐 Book Here:

M VILLAGE Tôn Thất Đạm

For those seeking a peaceful retreat amidst the city buzz, M Village is your haven. Tucked away in a quieter part of the city, it is still within reach of the Saigon Opera House, where you can enjoy a night of culture and music. The nearby Notre-Dame Cathedral, a stunning example of French colonial architecture, is worth a visit too. At the hotel's restaurant, don't miss the Bun Bo Hue, a spicy beef noodle soup that will tantalize your taste buds. Oh and did I mention they have a rooftop pool?

Budget: $$
Where: District 1   **Book Here:**

THE LIKE HOSTEL & CAFE

Okay coffee freaks. This is where you want to stay. Begin your day with a cup of traditional Vietnamese iced coffee at their on-site cafe, accompanied by a Banh Mi sandwich, a local favorite. The hostel is just a short walk from the War Remnants Museum, an absolute must-visit for history buffs. When night falls, the Ben Thanh Night Market is just right around the corner and comes alive with stalls selling everything from Pho to Goi Cuon (spring rolls), making it a foodie's paradise. The hostel prides itself on its cleanliness and safety, so you can rest easy after your city adventures.

Budget: $
Where: District 1   **Book Here:**

BUI VIEN STREET HOSTEL

Party girls, are you ready to go out for a night of wild antics on Bui Vien street? You'll meet other travelers here on the rooftop, end up going out for a beer and then wind up staying out till 3am. When you come back, you'll crawl into your luxury dorm bed with a privacy curtain and an outlet to charge your dying phone. Take your hangover downstairs in the morning for free breakfast and lots of water. When you're ready to carry on from the party life, the front desk is so helpful in booking tours and will help you sort out any visas for Vietnam and beyond!

Budget: $ **Where:** District 1   **Book Here:**

CHAPTER 13: HO CHI MINH CITY

Where to Eat in Ho Chi Minh City

BRUNCH IN HO CHI MINH CITY

Ho Chi Minh City's weather makes it the perfect brunch destination. You can certainly plop down in a plastic stool and enjoy a bowl of pho with the locals. Just look on any street corner or alley between the hours of 7am-11am and you'll find some pho to rock your world.

But when you're in the mood for a more international brunch or a brunch with some pizazz, here you go…

THE WORKSHOP

Out of all the cafes on this list, The Workshop will definitely be the busiest—and for good reason! This industrial-themed spot is a hit with young Vietnamese students and professionals. While it isn't the spot for a cozy morning read, it's a great option to get a few hours of laptop work or journaling. Its social atmosphere paired with Australia-grade coffee make it a must-do for any digital nomad.

Open: 8am-9am
Where: District 1
Address: 27 Ngo Duc Ke Street

PROPAGANDA BISTRO RESTAURANT

The murals that decorate Propaganda Bistro are all inspired by traditional Vietnamese propaganda posters. It's a journey back in time that also offers some tasty breakfast options- both Vietnamese and western. This place is so popular for their decor; however, I'm surprised they haven't stopped selling food and switched to just charging visitors for selfies. Enjoy the controversial vintage vibes and local cuisine before heading for a post-brunch stroll in the park across the street.

Open: 7:30am – 11pm
Where: District 1

THE HUNGRY PIG

This little hole in the wall has managed to bring a bit of England to southern Vietnam- seamlessly. You'll see what I mean with the Full English Breakfast that comes complete with all the fixins'. Just remember to come hungry because the portion sizes are more Western than they are Asian.

Open: 7am-9pm
Where: Pham Ngu Lao Ward
Address: 144 Cong Quynh Street

THE VINTAGE EMPORIUM ĐA KAO

Brunch is all about easing into your day. But when you're surrounded by countless motorbikes and car horns, that can be hard to do. Luckily, the Vintage Emporium serves as an oasis, with some of the most calming vibes in all of Saigon. They offer traditional brunch dishes that are affordable and delicious. I recommend trying a chocolate banana smoothie...or mimosas (because vacation)!

Open: 7am-9pm
Where: Near the Vietnam History Museum

LUNCH & DINNER IN HCMC

If you're anything like me, your days are saved for adventuring. You may start the morning off trekking through Saigon, exploring its hidden alleyways and markets. Afterwards, you'll have a massive afternoon filled with plans for museum visits and taking in the sites. Hitting up some of the town's best bars may even be in order to celebrate a day well done! But somewhere in between, you'll need to recharge and regroup. Where better than the perfect lunch spot?

POKE SAIGON

As you may have picked up by now, Saigon is the place where worlds clash—old and new, Western culture and Eastern culture, and so on. And when it comes to Poke Saigon, that remains true. This lunch spot offers a fascinating blend of Japanese and Hawaiian flavors in a Vietnamese setting. Plus, it's a good idea to get your fill of veggies and vitamins in between all the bread, noodles, and pork you'll be consuming during your gallivant around the country.

Open: 10am- 9pm
Where: District 1 (near the river)

DEN LONG - HOME COOKED VIETNAMESE RESTAURANT

Backpackers are always looking for the "authentic" travel experience. Most want to veer off the beaten path, finding new dives that offer meals the way the locals like them. And while Den Long is becoming popular with tourists, its homemade Vietnamese food is based on generations of traditional recipes. Better yet, the staff are always available to answer your questions about how the food is made and the cultural significance of each dish. It's a lesson and a meal in one!

⊙ **Open:** 11:00 - 22:00
♥ **Where:** District 1

PIZZA 4P'S (BEN THANH)

Somehow, the best pizza outside of Italy is in Vietnam! With locations in Ho Chi Minh City, Da Nang, and Hanoi, don't be surprised when I suggest this place over and over again- it's just that good! The pizza is mind-blowing with the highest quality ingredients around. Their specialty? Pizzas served with a fist-sized ball of mozzarella that is opened up like a blooming flower at the table, giving each bite of pizza the freshest touch.

PRO TIP! On the weekend, you'll likely need a reservation. Call ahead and request a seat near the oven so you can watch the magic happen.

⊙ **Open:** 10am - 10:30pm
♥ **Where:** District 1
🏠 **Address:** 8/15 Lê Thánh Tô

THE CHOPSTICKS SAIGON RESTAURANT

Just finding The Chopsticks Saigon Restaurant is an adventure. Located at the end of an obscure alley and quite easy to miss...you probably won't notice where to go until an usher calls you in, directing you to your table (they're used to it). The menu is full of elevated Vietnamese dishes, made by professional chefs in a clean kitchen with gourmet ingredients. For a unique take on a Vietnamese staple, try their coconut rice!

⊙ **Open:** 11:30am - 10:30pm
♥ **Where:** District 3

While these restaurants are to die for...most of the dinner magic in Saigon happens at the night markets. Keep reading...

STREET FOOD & NIGHT MARKETS

Pick any street, alley, neighborhood, or living room and you're sure to find someone cooking! Saigon is basically one giant kitchen. Whether you're on a tipsy night out or simply on your own street food tour, this is where some of the tastiest action is at.

The best way to get to know a new city - especially one as big and busy as Saigon - is through a food tour. Food is the door to everything in Vietnam: culture, history and social life. With a guide, you'll not only learn how to navigate street food, but also how to navigate the streets! Start your trip with the tours listed in the beginning of this chapter.

VAN KIEP STREET

Van Kiep Street is, by far, one of the best spots in all of Saigon to sample all the Vietnamese food your heart desires. Rain or shine, the street is bustling with food vendors. It's a super long street littered with neon signs advertising everything from Pho to more bizarre treats like crickets and larva. Better yet, it's situated directly between Phu Nhuan and Bin Thang Districts — two of the liveliest nightlife spots in town. Just keep in mind that you'll have around 100 vendors to choose from, so don't settle on the first stall you see!

⊙Open: Evening to Late
♥Where: Phu Nhuan District / Bin Thanh District

TRAN KHAC CHAN STREET

If Vietnamese street food is meant to do anything, it's to overwhelm your senses! And if you want Saigon's best sensory overload, Tran Khac Chan Street is the place to be. Motorbikes, cars, foreigners, locals, street vendors, and restaurants stretch as far as the eye can see. It's madness. Despite being no longer than two-hundred meters, over 50 street vendors pack themselves into every available space. Just follow your nose and eyes and eat spontaneously.

⊙Open: Evening to Late
♥Where: District 3

VINH KHANH STREET

Vinh Khanh is unique. It's extremely popular with young Vietnamese locals and is rumored to be popular with mafia members (don't worry, this strangely keeps the streets safer in terms of pickpockets). What makes this night market so unique is the representation of South Korea and Japan's hottest shopping trends AND the plethora of University students that descend on the abundance of cheap eats. Pull up a plastic stool, crack open some crab legs, and enjoy a cold beer amongst the madness.

⊙ **Open:** Evening to Late
📍 **Where:** Binh Thanh District

MINH PHUNG / CAY GO NIGHT MARKET

Minh Phung Night Market is known to many locals and expats as Cay Go Night Market. While many of Saigon's night markets occupy entire streets, Minh Phung weaves in and out of alleyways. It can feel like a maze after a while, which adds to the excitement of bartering and finding the best deals you can! Expect vendors selling everything from cheap t-shirts to hair ties and bracelets. A few vendors will have food, but this night market is definitely a shopping experience more than it is a culinary adventure.

⊙ **Open:** 2pm-Midnight
📍 **Where:** District 6

CHAPTER 13: HO CHI MINH CITY

Bars & Nightlife in Ho Chi Minh City

PASTEUR STREET BREWING COMPANY

American craft brewing meets local Vietnamese ingredients to make the best craft beer in the country. From IPAs to seasonal batches, you can find all the flavors of high-quality craft beer right here in Vietnam. Head to their most popular tap room and mingle with expats, tourists and locals. You'll also find Pasteur Street beers sold in restaurants all over Vietnam- so, if you don't get a chance to make it here, keep an eye out as you dine up and down the country.

☉ **Open:** Daily 11am - 11pm
📍**Where:** District 1 - in the Alley Next to the Rex Hotel

They've got more tap rooms sprinkled around the city. Check them out here: pasteurstreet.com/taprooms/

MARY JANE'S THE BAR

Rooftop real estate with basement prices! Mary Jane's offers 360 sweeping views of Saigon, plus one of the best seats in the city to witness the gorgeous sunset. All seating is outdoors where you catch a cool breeze while sipping on cold beer and fresh mojitos. To add a little mystery to the magic, Mary Jane's is a hidden spot with no signs. Enter a tall bank building and take the elevator to the roof. This is as local as it gets. Just show up to the address below and you'll figure it out.

☉**Open:** Daily 9am - 11:30pm
☆ **Happy Hour:** 10am – 12pm = 60k Mojitos
📍**Where:** District 3
♥ @maryjanes.thebar

MY HOUSE BAR AND CAFÉ

If you're looking for a more intimate experience, My House is the place to be. Living up to its name, this bar truly makes you feel like you're at home. The bartenders are among the most talented in all of Saigon, making cocktails that certainly stand out in a crowd. Some of the most charming customers even enjoy drinks invented specifically for them! Stop by in the early evening for a post-dinner cocktail and snack. It's a great spot to grab drinks before heading out for a night on the town.

Open: 11am- 1am
Where: District 1
@myhousehcmc

TNR SAIGON

Dive bar, anyone? TNR Saigon is the Saigon's best hole in the wall! option for anyone craving a unique bar experience. The atmosphere is lighthearted and fun, yet underground and urban. It serves as the perfect escape from the backpacker bars and clubs, featuring old school hip hop in place of pop and house. Better yet, the drinks are cheap!! If cool underground vibes are what you're after, you've found it.

Open: 6pm-5am
Where: District 1
@tnrsaigon

FUN FACT! Coffee culture is such a big deal in Ho Chi Minh City, that even businessmen close business deals in coffee shops.

CHAPTER 13: HO CHI MINH CITY

History & Culture in Ho Chi Minh City

Ho Chi Minh City is known for its endless war museums and sites. In fact, it's a shame to visit Saigon and not spend at least a day immersing yourself in the war that defined so much of the country's history. Join us in taking a break from urban exploring and day drinking to learn more about where Vietnam has been and where it's going!

CU CHI TUNNELS

The Cu Chi Tunnels are one of the most powerful Vietnam War sites you can visit while in Saigon. They're a true testament to how creative and determined Vietnamese troops were when it came to winning the war. You'll crawl through dark, winding tunnels to reach hidden rooms and storage space. You'll see the terrifying traps the Vietnamese relied on to fend off opposing troops. You'll even get the chance to try the wartime staples Vietnamese troops relied on to survive. And the few meters you explore will leave you wondering what life was like full-time in the tunnel network that spans over one-hundred kilometers.

💰 **Budget:** 110k Admissions (+90k if you opt for a tour)
🕒 **Open:** 7am – 5pm

WAR REMNANTS MUSEUM

Come prepared with some tissue, patience, and an open mind. This isn't going to be easy- particularly for Americans. When it comes to war, it's easy to imagine that it's all over when the shooting stops. However, the effects of the Vietnam War are still visible in Vietnam today. Even new generations — born decades after the war's end — are still facing the consequences. The War Remnants Museum highlights important details and events during the war in addition to its aftermath. Several exhibits are centered around photographing, highlighting everything from the terror of napalm bombs to the crippling effects of agent orange. It's an intense, sobering experience, but one that everyone in Saigon should have.

Budget: $.60 USD/ 15k VND
Open: 7:30 - 18:00
Where: District 3

REUNIFICATION PALACE

If you thought this name would be self-explanatory, you were right! The Reunification Palace is the site of the end of the Vietnam War. Here, the North Vietnamese Army officially captured Saigon and reunited the country under communist rule. Today, you can stroll through the peaceful gardens and visit small exhibits on the reunification of Vietnam. You'll also have the chance to see the various wartime rooms housed in the Palace, including bunkers and the commander's office. While it's not the most in-depth tour on our list, it's worth a stop simply because its front gates were seen by millions across the globe in 1975.

Budget: 40k Admission
Open: 7:30am – 11pm, 1pm - 4pm
Where: District 1

CHUA VAN PHAT – THE TEMPLE OF 10,000 BUDDHAS

I know, I know. If you've spent any more than a few days in Southeast Asia, then you've probably had your fill of temples! They seem to be everywhere and after a while they may all blur together. But I promise, Chua Van Phat will definitely stand out! It's a simple, charming pagoda in the middle of an extremely residential community. That alone makes it a great escape from the hustle and bustle of Saigon, allowing you to collect your thoughts before heading back into the madness. Even better, it boasts 10,000 small Buddha statues in a single room, which is truly a sight to behold. Now used exclusively by local families, this Pagoda is as off-the-beaten-path as you can get!

Budget: Free
Open: Sunrise to Sunset
Where: District 5 (Corner of Cach Mang Thang Tam & Nguyen Dinh Chieu Street)

THE VENERABLE THICH QUANG DUC MONUMENT

During the Vietnam War, protest both within the country and internationally was common. Students picketed and walked out of class. Families boycotted certain protections. Politicians called on the United States to pull out of the war. But the most shocking and extreme protests came in the form of self-immolation. At this street corner, a Vietnamese Monk chose to douse himself in petrol before setting himself on fire to protest the treatment of Buddhist Monks at the time. This monument was later created in his honor and sits at the corner of two of Saigon's busy, bustling streets. The contrast between peace, history, and urban life is clearer here than anywhere else in the city.

Budget: Free
Open: Always
Where: District 3 (Corner of Cach Mang Thang Tam & Nguyen Dinh Chieu Street)

HO CHI MINH SQUARE

Ho Chi Minh Square is in the dead-center of Saigon's busy District 1. Surrounded on all four sides by colonial buildings in the traditional French style, the square itself and a statue of its namesake are popular photo-ops for countless tourists. Historically, the square is home to Saigon's City Hall as well as the Rex Hotel, which housed international journalists throughout the Vietnam War. And once you've finished being a tourist, you can head on over to its modern shopping mall that comes equipped with a food court and the international stores you've come to love!

Budget: Free
Open: Always
Where: District 1

MUSEUM OF VIETNAMESE HISTORY

When you think of Vietnam, you most likely think of its civil war that drew international outcry. And that's entirely fair. The country we know today was born out of the war. However, Vietnam has centuries of interesting history — everything from Chinese imperial rule to French colonization. All together, that history explains a variety of things that make Vietnam so amazing (including why it's the only Southeast Asian country with great bread)! Spending a few hours at the Museum of Vietnamese History will help you learn how Vietnam came to be prior to the Communist takeover.

Budget: 15k Admission (+25k Fee to Photograph)
Open: 8am - 11:30am & 1:30pm – 5pm
Where: District 1

CHAPTER 13: HO CHI MINH CITY

Fun Things to Do in Ho Chi Minh City

DAY TRIP CAN GIO ISLANDS (MONKEY ISLAND)

During the Vietnam War, the Can Gio Islands were heavily hit by Agent Orange. Despite countless forests being knocked out, a newly formed nature reserve allows crocodiles and monkeys to thrive. It's an awesome opportunity to wade through the mangroves and experience tropical wildlife. Even better, you can go relax on one of several gorgeous beaches when you've had enough adventure for the day!

📍 **How to get there:** It's best to join a tour.

VISIT THE WATER PUPPET SHOW

Admittedly, this one sounds a bit lame – but I promise it's not! However, it makes for an awesome night and provides some insight into Vietnamese culture. This traditional show covers a variety of aspects of Vietnamese life, making it a great intro to Saigon. All of the puppets are controlled under the water, and they reveal the secret trick that makes it all work towards the end of the show.

💵**Budget:** 230k
🕐**Open:** Shows at 6:30pm and 8:30pm
📍**Where:** District 1

PRO TIP! Get your ticket ahead of time to skip the line:

VISIT BITEXCO FINANCIAL TOWER

Unless you're a regular at sky bars, you probably haven't seen Ho Chi Minh City from the sky. On the street, it's easy to feel trapped in the moment. Cars and motorbikes combine with the humidity to overwhelm your senses, leaving you dazed and a bit confused. But with a quick elevator ride to an aerial viewpoint, you'll feel like those cars are just ants. It's nothing short of amazing to see the city's big picture for once! Better yet, you'll also get a quick cultural lesson thanks to a small exhibit on traditional Vietnamese dress.

Budget: 200k
Open: 9:30am – 9:30pm
Where: District 1

HIRE A MOTO-TAXI

Do I recommend driving in Ho Chi Minh City? Definitely not! Saigon boasts some of the craziest traffic in the world, boasting nearly as many motorbikes as people. However, you can't go through Saigon without hopping on the back of a motorbike at least once. Trust the pros to drive; it's such a thrilling experience. And with Grab Taxi, it's never been easier!

Budget: 10k-30k
Open: Always
Where: Anywhere (I recommend District 1)

FUN FACT! The Vietnamese alphabet has 29 letters instead of 26, and it's a unique combination of the latin alpahbet and added letters.

CHAPTER 13: HO CHI MINH CITY

Markets & Shopping in Ho Chi Minh City

Malls, markets, street vendors, and more! If you're a shopaholic, Saigon is the place for you. Ho Chi Minh City definitely doesn't have a shortage of shopping opportunities. From knock-off handbags at bargain prices to luxury goods at top-end retailers, you're sure to find what you're looking for. Why not get some holiday shopping done while you're in town? Put that VAT refund to good use!

BEN THANH MARKET

The OG of hawker markets. You can find literally everything and anything in Ben Thanh. It's the most popular market in HCMC because of its central location in District 1 and its abundance of goodies. Just be prepared for lots of women vendors shouting "Buy something, lady" around every corner with their calculator in hand. Haggle, shop around, and don't feel pressured to buy shit if you don't want to.

⊙**Open:** Early morning – 7pm (then the outside turns into a night market)
Where: District 1

VINCOM CENTER

The Vincom Center is possibly Saigon's most popular shopping mall. If you've had your fill of outdoor markets, the air-con and brand name stores will be a pleasant change of pace. You'll find everything from cell phone accessories to clothing. Once you've shopped your heart out, be sure to check out the food court. Even though you'd imagine food courts are unchanged internationally, the Vietnamese have added their own twists at every corner!

⊙ **Open:** 9am-10pm
📍 **Where:** District 1

STREET SHOPPING

Saigon is home to countless streets solely dedicated to shopping. There are too many to list them all, but three destinations definitely stand out. First off, Le Van Sy Street is home to endless street vendors selling everything from clothes to bed sheets at insanely low prices. Next, Nguyen Trai Street boasts one of the busiest shopping districts in town, with countless boutique stores and haggle-friendly vendors. Lastly, Nguyen Dinh Chieu Street is locally known as the place to purchase great and affordable shoes (just keep in mind that Western sizes won't always be available).

HANH THONG TAY NIGHT MARKET

Unlike many other night markets, Hanh Thong Tay doesn't boast a lot of food. Instead, it's the perfect stop to find cheap bags, clothes, cosmetics, and more. It's especially popular with Saigon's university students, giving it a uniquely youthful vibe. This market is essentially your one-stop shop — I promise you'll be able to find anything you're looking for! And while it's not the best spot for food, the portions are big and the prices low.

⊙ **Open:** 6pm – 11pm
📍 **Where:** Go Vap District

CHAPTER 13: HO CHI MINH CITY

How to Get Around Ho Chi Minh City

WALK

You can walk everywhere during the day in Ho Chi Minh City, as long as you're mindful of traffic. However, please be cautious at night – particularly in District 1. There are bag snatchers, often on motorbikes looking for easy targets. Wear a cross-shoulder bag, especially when you're drinking.

GRAB TAXI

GrabBikes and taxis are everywhere! Grab Bikes costs around $1-$2 and GrabCars typically cost $2-$3 depending where you're going. Install this app ASAP.

TAXIS

I do not recommend getting in a taxi here. It's common for a taxi to charge you 100k for the same journey that a Grab Taxi would charge just 30K for. 3x the price, ya'll. If you have no choice, go with Mai Linh Taxi – they are the most trustworthy of the bunch.

SCOOTER

…if you dare. I'm an experienced driver and even I don't attempt to drive a scooter in this crazy city.

CHAPTER 13: HO CHI MINH CITY

From the Airport to Ho Chi Minh City

Almost every traveler starts their Vietnam adventure in HCMC. With super cheap flights from Bangkok and Phnom Penh, odds are that you'll fly in, too.

Once you're out of the airport, here's what you'll do next!

OPTION 1: GRAB TAXI

Once you're outside the airport, order a grab. They'll take you anywhere you need to go and help you with your bags.

Budget: Around $9 USD / 200k VND

Duration: 30-40 minutes

OPTION 2: THE BUS

Outside of the arrival hall, you can hop on a very cheap bus to District 1 (where most hostels and hotels are).

Look for bus Number 152.

You'll pay 5,000 dong for yourself and 5,000 dong for your bag.

You board, tell the driver "District 1", and he'll tell you when to get off. You'll likely see other backpackers doing the same- so if all else fails, you can just follow their lead.

The bus drops you off near Ben Thanh Market, not far from Boi Vien Street.

Budget: $0.23 USD / 5k VND

Duration: 55 minutes depending on traffic

Where: Right outside the terminal

When: Every day, every 15 minutes.

This bus stops running around 6pm.

HUGE PRO TIP! If for some reason you need to take a public taxi, ONLY ride with Mai Linh or Vinasun Taxi.

OPTION 3: PRIVATE TRANSFER

Melt your stress. It's worth a couple extra dollars.

TRAVEL NOTES:

....

....

....

....

....

MINI Directory
FOR VIETNAM

Police: 113   *Fire:* 114   *Ambulance – First Aid:* 115

EMBASSIES

British Embassy Hanoi
Phone: 024 3936 0500
Address: 4 Central Building, 31 Hai Bà Trưng, Tràng Tiền, Hoàn Kiếm, Hà Nội

British Consulate Ho Chi Minh City
Phone: 028 3825 1380
Address: 25 Lê Duẩn, Bến Nghé, District 1, Hồ Chí Minh

US Embassy Hanoi
Phone: 024 3850 5000
Address: Chợ Dừa, Ba Đình, Hà Nội

US Consulate Ho Chi Minh
Phone: 028 3520 4200
Address: 4 Lê Duẩn, Bến Nghé, Quận 1, Hồ Chí Minh

Canadian Embassy Hanoi
Phone: 024 3734 5000
Address: 31 Hùng Vương, Điện Bàn, Ba Đình, Hà Nội

Canadian Consulate Ho Chi Minh
Phone: 028 3827 9899
Address: The Metropolitan, 235 Đồng Khởi, Bến Nghé, Quận 1, Hồ Chí Minh

South African Embassy Hanoi
Phone: 024 3936 2000
Address: 31 Hai Bà Trưng, Hàng Bài, Hoàn Kiếm, Hà Nội

South African Consulate Ho Chi Minh
Phone: 028 3823 8556
Address: 80 Võ Văn Tần, Phường 6, Quận 3, Hồ Chí Minh

Australian Embassy Hanoi
Phone: 024 3774 0100
Address: Đào Tấn, Cống Vị, Ba Đình, Hà Nội

Australian Consulate Ho Chi Minh
Phone: 028 3521 8100
Address: 45 Lý Tự Trọng, Bến Nghé, Quận 1, Hồ Chí Minh

GYNECOLOGY SERVICES & FEMALE STUFF

Birth Control Pills

You can buy birth control pills and contraception over the counter in Vietnam. The word for birth control in Vietnamese is "thuốc tránh thai".

Some of the most popular brands include HN Choice, Rigevidon, Marvelon, and Microgynon – you can do an easy search for these pills online.

Morning After Pill

All pharmacies carry the Morning After Pill for around $2. There are at least 9 different brands, all of which you can take within a 120-hour window after unprotected sex.

Depo Shot / IUDs

You can get the Depo shot for as low as $15 and the IUD for $150-$350... without insurance. For these, you can visit one of the gynecologists we've listed below.

WOMEN'S HEALTH CENTERS IN HANOI

→ Hanoi Family Program

→ The French Vietnamese Hospital

→ International SOS

→ Family Medical Practice

WOMEN'S HEALTH CENTERS HO CHI MINH

→ Family Medical Practice

→ International SOS

If you find yourself in an "accidental fertility situation" then visit Family Medical Practice Vietnam (Hanoi or Ho Chi Minh) to receive "Unwanted Pregnancy Pills". You'll have a consultation with a Women's Health Doctor, who will provide an exam and the pill for around $230 total.

Abortions are legal in Vietnam, up to 22 weeks. Check out France-Vietnam Hospital in HCMC or Family Medical Practice in both Hanoi and HCMC.

For more information, check out gynopedia.org/Vietnam

Please make sure you've come to Vietnam with Travel Insurance. If you don't have it yet, scan this code ☞

THE TRUE STORY OF HOW THE
Solo Girl's Travel Guide
WAS BORN

I was robbed in Sihanoukville.

Sure, the robber was a child and yes, I might have drunkenly put my purse down in the sand while flirting with an irresistible Swedish boy…but that doesn't change the fact that I found myself without cash, a debit card and hotel key at 1am in a foreign country.

My mini robbery, however, doesn't even begin to compare to my other travel misadventures. I've also been scammed to tears by taxi drivers, idiotically taken ecstasy in a country with the death penalty for drugs and missed my flight because how was I supposed to know that there are two international airports in Bangkok?

It's not that I'm a total idiot.
It's just that…people aren't born savvy travelers.

I'm not talking about hedonistic vacationers who spend their weekend at a resort sipping Mai Tais. I'm talking about train-taking, market-shopping, street food-eating travelers!

Traveling is not second (or third or fourth) nature; it's a skill that only comes with sweaty on-the-ground experience…especially for women!

In the beginning of my travels (aka the first 5 years), I made oodles of travel mistakes. And thank god I did. These mistakes eventually turned me into the resourceful, respected and established travel guru that I am today.

Year-after-year and country-after-country, I started learning things like...

✓ Always check your hostel mattress for bed bugs.

✓ Local alcohol is usually toxic and will give you a hangover that lasts for days.

✓ The world isn't "touristy" once you stop traveling like a tourist.

✓ And most importantly, the best noodle shops are always hidden in back alleys.

After nearly 11 years of traveling solo around the world (4 continents and 26 countries, but who's counting?) – I travel like a gosh darn pro. I save money, sleep better, haggle harder, fly fancier, and speak foreign languages that help me almost almost blend in with the locals despite my blonde hair.

Yeah yeah yeah. I guess it's cool being a travel icon. But shoot...

Do you know how much money, how many panic attacks, and how many life-threatening risks I could have saved and/or avoided if only someone had freakin' queued me into all of this precious information along the way? A lot. A lotta' lot.

So, why didn't I just pick up a travel guide and start educating myself like an adult? I had options...right? I could've bought a copy of Lonely Planet... but how the hell am I supposed to smuggle a 5-pound brick in my carry-on bag? Or DK Eyewitness, perhaps? Hell no. I don't have 8 hours to sift through an encyclopedia and decode details relevant to my solo adventure.

There was no travel guide that would have spared my tears or showed me how to travel safer and smarter.

The book I needed didn't exist. So, I freakin' wrote it myself.

What travel guide do you need me to write next?

Tell me on Instagram ♥ @SoloGirlsTravelGuide

THE 11 TRAVEL COMMANDMENTS
OF THE Solo Girl's Travel Guide

01 BE AN EXPLORER, NOT A TOURIST.

Some people travel just for the photo. While others travel to find the unfamiliar, connect with strangers, expand their minds, and try new things for the sake of trying new things. Which kind of traveler are you?

02 LEAVE ROOM FOR HAPPENSTANCE

Don't overstuff your itinerary. Slow down, be where you are and leave room for serendipity! Literally, schedule serendipity time so the universe can take the lead.

03 VOTE WITH YOUR DOLLAR

When possible, choose to support local businesses that operate ethically - aka businesses that respect the environment, benefit their local communities, don't take advantage of animals and just treat their staff really really well.

04 LOOK FOR THE GIFT

Love your mistakes! With every bump in the road comes a gift. Miss a bus? Look for the gift. Lose your room key? Look for the gift. Get dumped on your honeymoon? Look for the gift! There will always be a gift.

05 STAY CURIOUS

Ask questions! Ask questions when you like something and ask questions when you don't understand something. Out loud or in your head. And whenever you feel judgment arise, replace it with a question instead.

06 MORE STORIES, LESS PHOTOS

Take a couple photos and then put your phone away. While everyone else is taking shitty sunset photos that never look as good on camera…you are really there, experiencing every shade of color in real time. Take note in your head of the story you will bring home - of the people you see, the food you smell, the monkeys in the trees! Look up, not down.

07 COUNT EXPERIENCES, NOT PASSPORT STAMPS

You can never "do" Cambodia. You can go to Cambodia 50 times and still each experience will be different than the last. Travel to live, not to brag.

08 MIND YOUR IMPACT

Leave every place better than you found it. Take a piece of trash from the beach and be kind to people you meet. Bring your own water bottle, canvas bag, and reusable straw to avoid single-use plastics.

09 AVOID VOLUNTOURISM

People are not zoo animals. Playing with children at orphanages, temporarily teaching English in villages or volunteering at women's shelters hurt more than they help. Want to volunteer with a positive impact? Check out my blog at Alexa-West.com

10 CARRY YOUR POSITIVITY

Ever had a crappy day and then a stranger smiles at you and flips your entire mood? Travel can be hard, but your positivity will be your secret weapon. Happy vibes are contagious. Even when we don't speak the local language, a smile or a random act of kindness tips the universal scale in the right direction for you and the people you meet along your journey.

11 TRUST YOUR GUT

Listen to that little voice inside you. When something doesn't feel right, back away. When something feels good, lean. Your intuition will lead you to beautiful places, unforgettable moments, and new lifelong friends.

BONUS: Drink where the Locals Drink, Eat Where the Locals Eat

Even if it's under a tarp outside a mini mart. This is how you discover the best food and make the most meaningful connections.

It feeeeeeeels good to travel good.

A CONFESSION:

I bend the rules. Sometimes I stay in an all-inclusive resort instead of a locally owned guesthouse. Sometimes I go to McDonalds because I want a taste of home. And sometimes, especially when I'm tired or hungry, I'm not all sunshine and rainbows to be around.

But my moral travel compass does not bend for things that matter to me. I'll never leave a piece of trash on the beach. I'll never support elephant riding. I'd rather stay home than go on a Carnival Cruise even if it was free. Decide what matters to you now, let that guide you as you travel but let yourself be human.

Comfort yourself when you need comforting and eat the forbidden fruit sparingly. When you do make mistakes, brush yourself off and do better next time. No one's path is perfect but I'm proud of you for making your path better.

THIS TRIP.

THIS IS WHEN YOU DISCOVER EXACTLY WHO YOU ARE.

TRUST YOURSELF.

DO YOU HAVE THIS BOOK YET?

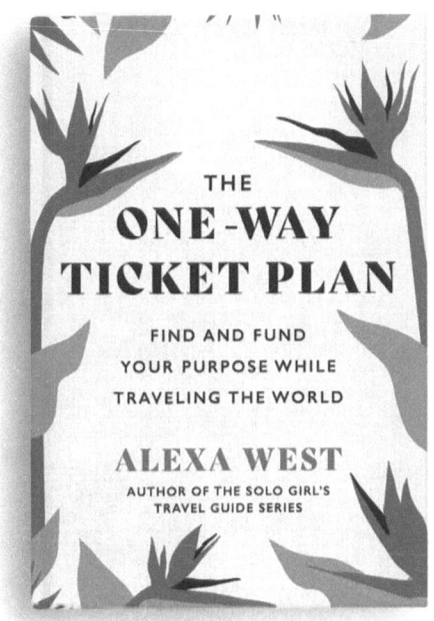

THE ONE-WAY TICKET PLAN

FIND AND FUND YOUR PURPOSE WHILE TRAVELING THE WORLD

....

GET IT AT ALEXA-WEST.COM

....

Did you know everything Solo Girl's Travel Guide is made by just two girls?

That's right, just me and my #TravelBFF Emy. We do all the research, traveling, writing, editing, fact checking, designing...No fancy publishers, just the two of us here.

You an also follow our adventures on Insta as we create more books for you.

@sologirlstravelguide | @__helloemilia

LOVE THIS BOOK?
Please leave us a review!

As a self-published author –
doing this whole publishing thing by myself –
reviews are what keeps
The Solo Girl's Travel Guide growing.

Your review helps other girls find this book
and experience a truly life-changing trip.

Ps. We read every single review.

Room for improvement?
Please email us and tell us how we can make this
book even better!

✉ hello@thesologirlstravelguide.com

PASS IT ON!

This guidebook is meant to change lives.
Don't let it sit on a shelf forever and ever.

Before you give this book to a friend
who needs a travel push
or before you leave it in the hostel
for the next travel girl to find…

On the back cover…

✧ write your name,
✧ your Instagram,
✧ and the dates you traveled.

This is your legacy, too.

xoxo, Alexa

WHERE NEXT?

BALI

THAILAND

MEXICO CITY

SOUTH KOREA

PUERTO VALLARTA

CAMBODIA

And More...

Get The Whole Collection.

www.ingramcontent.com/pod-product-compliance
Lightning Source LLC
Chambersburg PA
CBHW020301010526
44108CB00037B/278